"Sara Arnell is the only writer I know who can make self-deprecation and wisdom look like the same thing. *There Will Be Lobster* is a darkly funny memoir with a big heart, and it's the exact comeback story we all need right now."

—DAVID HOLLANDER, author of *Anthropica* and *L.I.E.*

"No matter where you are in life's journey, there are stories and anecdotes in this book that will confirm what we know but don't always practice—self-care and self-love are the two most powerful healers you have available."

—DR. GABRIELLE LYON

"This book is a deeply personal story that's not afraid to show you the crazy moments that we all have, but often don't admit to. Read this memoir if you want to learn how honesty, vulnerability, and sheer perseverance can help you step into your light and illuminate a new path—one that is happy, healthy, and full of hope."

—ANDRÉ LEON TALLEY, author of *New York Times* bestseller, *The Chiffon Trenches* and former *Vogue* editor-at-large

"Reading this book makes you want to look more closely at your friendships, ask more real questions, and take the time to truly pay attention to signs and signals that indicate a friend needs help. *There Will Be Lobster* is a poignant portrayal of a woman in crisis—a woman like many of us—so used to being the strong one at home and work, that she just doesn't know how to ask for help. It's a must read for anyone who is looking to make a transition to a new chapter in their life."

—CHRISTINA JUAREZ, CEO, CJ & Company

"This is Sara's story, in her own words of how she stepped into her light and illuminated a magical, better world for herself. It's a crazy ride, full of extraordinary characters and events but in the end, her compelling honesty is a lesson in how to help heal yourself and be the best you can be."

—ALYSSA DUFFY, founder, a-listed studio

"What an enjoyable read. Sara gives us quite a ride upon the wave of elevational theater in her study of the futility of chasing lasting happiness solely in its external reflections. After decades of winning deserved accolades, Sara's belief in herself reaches its lowest ebb when, unexpectedly, she discovers through Vedic Meditation how to turn within and finds what she was seeking: inner contentedness and purpose. Sara skillfully and courageously shares her life experiences with candor and humor. In doing so, she exemplifies a Vedic principle of good citizenship, to make personal experiences relevant socially, thereby making one's growth toward illumination relatable, bringing hope to readers."

—THOM KNOLES, Vedic Meditation Master

"While names and storylines may differ, Sara's intimate account of her transformation from seeking fulfillment through others to ultimately finding it within herself is a journey of awakening we all find ourselves on. Through Sara's masterful storytelling, we can see that even in moments of struggle, loss, and fear, life will hand us breadcrumbs of hope that encourage us to continue searching for a better way. Regardless of where you are on your journey, Sara's story will inspire you to take that next step in realizing your full potential and purpose, with some laughs along the way."

—SUSAN CHEN, founder, Meditate With Susan

"Sara Arnell's memoir *There Will Be Lobster* is filled with wry self-deprecating humor but equally replete with genuine poignancy. In writing so transparently about the full catastrophe of her midlife crisis, Sara takes us on a journey that arrives at hard-earned resilience and lasting insight. This book is a rollicking account of the human condition written in an authentic, original voice."

—GAIL STRAUB, co-founder, Empowerment Institute
and award-winning author *Empowerment* and *The Ashokan Way*

"I remember Sara Arnell as the tough, polished woman wearing a perfectly chic leather jacket while ruling over the hottest branding agency in Manhattan. Through *There Will Be Lobster*, I met a frightened, bewildered woman lurching through a terribly dark midlife passage. That both people are the same shows how sharply life can change. Sara shows that our only chance is changing with it—and that change is a messy, frightening process best handled with brutal honesty and humor."

—HUGH O'NEIL GALLAGHER, brand writer and author, *Chicken 65*

...IFE CRISIS

THERE WILL BE LOBSTER

SARA ARNELL

SAVIO
REPVBLIC

A SAVIO REPUBLIC BOOK
An Imprint of Post Hill Press

There Will Be Lobster:
Memoir of a Midlife Crisis
© 2021 by Sara Arnell
All Rights Reserved

ISBN: 978-1-64293-926-2
ISBN (eBook): 978-1-64293-927-9

Cover art by Cody Corcoran

posthillpress.com
New York • Nashville

Published in the United States of America
1 2 3 4 5 6 7 8 9 10

To my children

CONTENTS

*Learn How to Change Your Life and Achieve
the Success You Desire!* ix

Chapter 1: January 1, 2015 1

Chapter 2: How Did We Miss an Eighteen-Pound Tumor? 6

Chapter 3: Spring 2013 12

Chapter 4: Levon Helm Is in the Hospital 15

Chapter 5: Grandpa, Is that You? 20

Chapter 6: The Cautionary Tail 33

Chapter 7: Goodbye to All This 37

Chapter 8: Listen to the Music Play 43

Chapter 9: The Gimp Is Back 46

Chapter 10: You Look Like Joni Mitchell 50

Chapter 11: Home Alone 55

Chapter 12: Please Don't Die 58

Chapter 13: Gone But Not Forgotten 60

Chapter 14: Smile Therapy 68

Chapter 15: The Medium 76

Chapter 16: Step Over the Log 80

Chapter 17: Psychic-Ology 82

Chapter 18: Crying at the Gym 86

Chapter 19: Cat's out of the Bag 90

Chapter 20: You Must Change Your Life .92

Chapter 21: I'm Going Home 96

Chapter 22: Jesus Will Save You 103

Chapter 23: There Will Be Lobster. 107

Chapter 24: Just Breathe 112

Chapter 25: I Want to Come Home 124

Chapter 26: Turn Left 128

Chapter 27: It's Just a Cold. 134

Chapter 28: You Can Scream if You Want 139

Chapter 29: You're Going to do Great. 144

Chapter 30: Heal Yourself 147

Chapter 31: I Can Smell Cancer 152

Chapter 32: The Thing 155

Chapter 33: Into the Light 161

Acknowledgments. 164

LEARN HOW TO CHANGE YOUR LIFE
AND ACHIEVE THE SUCCESS YOU DESIRE!

Now that I have your attention by using the advertising skills I've honed over the past thirty years of work in the industry, I want to tell you a bit about what you'll encounter in this memoir. And maybe, just maybe, the promise of the headline will come true.

The journey you'll be going on in this book is driven by the things I did, thought and thought about over a several year period of disruptive life shifts, stifling anxiety, depression, and a jarring health diagnosis. It was a packed few years and it took a lot for me to unpack them and write them down. I had to face myself and what I did, *again*. It was hard enough the first time. The second time needed to be for reasons of lessons learned and shared.

Along the way, during the writing of this book, I spoke with a lot of people to help me remember clearly, get the sentiment right, and remind me of the moments I wanted—or tended—to forget. My description and explanation about this book was met with very similar responses:

"You have money and resources. Couldn't you get professional help?"

"What was your family doing to help you through this?"

"I never noticed you were having a hard time."

"Who knew?!?"

And I would answer…

"I couldn't buy myself happy, after a while. That I-bought-a-new-bag feeling didn't last very long. I rejected therapy because it felt like an insult to my intelligence."

"My family would say they thought I was just a little down and would perk up soon. A lot of internal stuff isn't always outwardly expressed. No one imagined I was beyond anything that a good night's sleep couldn't fix."

"I never talked about how bad I felt about myself. I got really good at hiding my behavior or chalking it up to feeling free instead of out of control and self-destructive. Basically, I lied about what I was doing and what it was doing to me."

"I went from a CEO to a CE-OH no she didn't. It surprised a lot of people."

But the reason I faced my bad, sad self a second time was because I learned some things that I want—need—to share. I know I'm not the only woman who has found herself in a midlife crisis of family, faith, and an uncertain future. I know I'm not the only woman who has had too much to drink and made decisions in the moment that didn't look quite as chill or fun or smart in the light of a new day. And I know that I'm not the only woman who has searched hard to figure things out, get things straight, set things right, and still struggle to find a way out of a gaping black hole.

In this book, you'll read a lot of stories and anecdotes that have become my life lessons. There are stories about an eighteen-pound tumor, a tailless cat, a dying rock star, a famous medium, and a former monk. I was obsessed with self-care and all its accoutrements—crystals, mala beads, facials, massages, healings—but could care less about my actual health and wellness, until a cancer diagnosis woke me up. I searched for signs from the afterlife as I missed sign after sign from the world around me. I was a creature of media and consumed sensational stories of death, murder, and criminal behavior that caused me to fear for my children and myself.

From boundless misplaced effort, false affirmations, self-pity, senseless worry, and the debilitating, utter depression of it all, I learned one huge lesson.

Okay. Spoiler alert. I know I'm about to give away the ending and the ah-ha moment I finally achieved, courtesy of the former monk, but what the heck. I would rather have you hear this now and not have to wait until the end of the book, because it's that urgent to know and put into practice.

I learned that nothing external changes for you unless things change inside you first. Or, said the more commonly quoted way:

"When things change inside you, things change around you."

This is the journey into light that we make on a daily basis through our decisions, actions, and thoughts. This is the acknowledgment that happiness exists inside you. It's not something you chase, buy, or conjure. It's something you tap into, deep inside yourself. When you do this, positive thoughts, laughter, joy, clarity, love, and hope all bubble up. Happiness is not on the other side of achievement. Happiness is what propels achievement. Finding what makes you healthy, happy, and whole is the horse, not the cart.

Watching a lobster crawl out from under a chair was the signal that I needed to change my life and come back into the world.

We all have lobster moments. Think about yours and how you can use it to change your life, from the inside out.

Love always. Always love.

Sara

CHAPTER 1

JANUARY 1, 2015

This morning was different. I couldn't wash it away.

My ritual of letting hot, soothing shower water stream down my back for an extra ten minutes before I stepped onto the plush bath mat to dry off would have to wait. The shower drain was clogged with vomit.

I achingly grunted, "Happy New Year" to myself as I tried to get up from my bathroom floor. I could barely move. Every part of my body hurt. I imagined this was what it would feel like if I ran a marathon. Or was in a car accident. Or fell down a flight of stairs. The pain started from the top of my head and extended down my entire body. There was not a bone, a muscle, a sinew left untouched or unaffected. I noticed that I was wearing my terrycloth bathrobe and that it was damp. "Oh God," I sighed as I struggled to my knees and wedged myself between the toilet and the sink. With my body in this semi-vertical position, I began to look around and assess the situation. Vomit covered the floor. The glass shower door was ajar. The toilet paper roll was in the tub. Something that may have been a towel or a slaughtered rabbit lay crumpled under the sink.

I was still on my knees, so I dropped my head and considered praying, except I didn't know what to pray for at this point. Should I pray for my headache to go away? That seemed selfish. Should I pray for a better year ahead, beginning with right now? That seemed too broad and not of the moment. Should I pray to be able to stand and get myself together for my children who were probably on their way to my house for a New Year's Day brunch? *Yes.* That was the prayer I needed answered.

I made it from my knees to the side of the tub and sat there for a few minutes hoping the dizziness would dissipate before I stood all the way up. Thirty minutes later, I had completed the journey from the floor to a standing position in front of my bathroom mirror. The face that stared back at me was almost unrecognizable. My hair was wet and hanging in front of my face with chunks of regurgitation falling to the floor like confetti as I brushed it back to reveal a big, black eye. On the other side of my face, my right cheek was bleeding. The skin was peeled and blistered. I had burned my face from lying wet on the radiant-heated tiles. I had no idea how long I had been on the bathroom floor or even what time it was. Panic began to set in. *I have to cook*, I reminded myself. *I have fifteen people here for brunch at 1:00 p.m.* I swallowed three Motrin and decided to lie down in my bed for a few minutes while they took effect. I brushed as much puke from my hair as I could and crept under the covers. I thought about taking another shower but couldn't bring myself to clear the clogged drain or rinse the glass walls that were dripping with projectile spew from hours prior.

"Mom!" was the distressed bellow I woke to.

"What time is it?"

"It's almost noon," said my daughter, standing parentally over my bed. "I came early to see if you needed any help."

"I'm so sorry. I am so, so sorry. I'll get up now."

My daughter helped me to the bathroom, which I had to clean before I could use. The smell was a putrid reminder of tequila shots.

I had a vague recollection of slamming my face on the toilet bowl as I was heaving into it. My son was home for the holiday from Utah, where he lived, and had about ten friends sleep over after spending New Year's Eve in New York City. They rolled in at about 4:00 a.m. *I remember popping bottles of champagne and doing shots. I remember noise and music and dancing on the large kitchen island. And then I remember waking up on my bathroom floor.*

By the time I made it downstairs, it was well after 1:00 p.m., and my daughter had left to eat somewhere else, realizing there would be no brunch. No one else in the house was awake. For that, I was thankful. *Maybe this is what I should pray for*, I thought, *that they sleep all day and that I don't have to cook and clean.* My head was still pounding. I sat at the kitchen table, which was strewn with remnants of our early morning party. Some of the food I had prepared the day before for brunch was already eaten. There would be no macaroni and cheese or crudité with dip. Or pie. There was no apple pie left. It was all eaten or destroyed or used for spontaneous sporting activities. I began to see food scattered on the walls and smeared on the countertops. *What the hell happened?* I shuffled to the counter and managed to put a pod in the Keurig to make a cup of coffee. While trying to keep my first sip down, I saw one of the slipcovers on the kitchen chairs move. I stared, wondering if it had really moved or if it was just my brain jumping inside my skull, causing me to see things. It moved again. One claw then another emerged, followed by a big, red body. I watched a lobster crawl out from under the chair.

I picked it up to put it back in the refrigerator and postpone its death by boiling indefinitely, only to find that the rest of the lobsters I was going to serve for brunch were no longer shifting about in the water of the holding tank. The pot on the stove, I guessed from a glance, was where I could find them. I wondered how this one had managed to escape whatever primal madness had overrun the kitchen. *This is a smart one*, I noted. I slid the chairs back from the table to see if there were more stray lobsters that needed to be rescued, but instead found piles of lobster shells that had been discarded, as if by starving castaways on a beach.

I took my coffee and went back to bed. I cried for the next few hours. I cried because I had failed as a mother. I cried because I had let my children down and missed a chance to celebrate with them and to spend time with family and friends. I cried because I had a black eye, a scalded cheek, a splitting headache, and an upset stomach—all self-inflicted and all because I'd been so determined to show my family that I was good, really good. I felt the need to prove that I was their happy-go-lucky, fun, cool-with-everything, nothing's-a-problem, glass-is-half-full, freedom-loving, young-at-heart, skinny-jean-wearing, better-than-ever mom. But I was the opposite of good. I was jobless, directionless, divorced, single, middle-aged, and the last of my three children had recently moved out for college. I was spinning through a gigantic, gaping hole into the deepest, darkest blackness that I had ever experienced. The starving castaway here was me, picking up lobster shells and sorting through them on a deserted kitchen island.

I knew I had died a thousand slow, painful deaths. I was no longer the woman, mother, friend, sister, or daughter I once was. I didn't recognize myself anymore. When I tried to be the chill mom, I landed with my head in the toilet bowl. When I tried to be badass, I ended up feeling mean and thoughtless (and was called the same). I wondered why I couldn't convince the universe to see all my potential and transform me into a new and improved version of myself. "Here I am, universe," I would say aloud. "Work your magic." But the universe had other plans. I was a fountain of self-pity, self-regret, and sorrow. I felt sorry for everyone who encountered me in this sad state. All I was putting into the world were forms of sorrow, and that's all I got back.

"It's understandable," people told me, "that you've lost your footing. Your life has been turned upside down." "You're an empty nester," I was reminded, like it was a kiss of death that only the brave and strong could survive without emotional trauma or alcohol abuse. But I knew it was more than being an "empty nester" that had me wallowing in self-pity, binging on hard liquor, and acting like nothing really mattered anymore. It was shame. I had failed everyone around me. I started almost every sentence with the words "I'm sorry." I ended almost every sentence with "I'm sorry." And I was sorry from start to finish, every day, for everything I said or did. How had I gotten here? It was time to trace that path and to figure out how (or if) I should go forward.

CHAPTER 2

HOW DID WE MISS
AN EIGHTEEN-POUND TUMOR?

"Mom. I have a terrible pain in my side. I've had it all day, and it's getting worse. I think I need to go to the hospital," my older daughter had texted.

It was fall of 2012—more than two years before the New Year's debacle—and I was in class at Sarah Lawrence College, working part-time on my master's degree. I left the classroom to respond to her 911 text. "I'll meet you at the emergency room. Can you drive, or are you in too much pain?" I asked.

"I can meet you there."

I walked into the emergency room entrance and saw her waiting nervously. I grabbed her hand, and we walked up to the front desk. I told the nurse on duty that we thought she was having an appendicitis attack. We had diagnosed this based on a Google search of "pain in lower right abdomen" and the fact that my younger daughter had had her appendix removed several years prior and the symptoms seemed the same. We were quickly taken inside and given a room. She changed into a hospital gown and we waited.

"I'm really scared," she said. "I need a hug."

"Don't worry," I said, while holding her tightly. "Getting your appendix out these days is a breeze. They do it with a laser. You won't even have a scar."

"Really?"

"Yeah. Don't worry."

The ER resident on duty came in after a few minutes and examined her. She told us they wanted to do an ultrasound to confirm that it was appendicitis.

"It's all going to be fine," I called out as she was wheeled away.

About thirty minutes after she was returned to her curtained-off room in the ER, the resident walked in and went directly to her. The doctor followed in slow motion, approaching my daughter's bed like a zombie, arms extended and head tilted to one side. She touched my daughter's shoulder and began rubbing it.

"I'm sorry," the doctor said.

My daughter and I burst into tears. We had no idea what she was "sorry" about, but we knew it couldn't be good. The doctor looked like she'd just seen a ghost—one that was living inside my child's body.

"What," I said, "what did you find on the ultrasound?"

"It's quite a large mass."

"What do you mean?"

"She has a large mass on top of her ovary."

"How large?"

"It's the biggest I've ever seen."

The doctor told us that my child needed surgery right away. I caught my breath and called my ob-gyn at NYU Hospital. I wanted him to look at the ultrasound and get his opinion before we made any decisions on surgery. I put him on the phone with the doctor, who informed him what was going on with my daughter. He told us to relax for the night, if possible, and to meet him the next morning at the hospital. He would put together a team of specialists and a top-notch surgeon, and the operation would take place the following afternoon.

My daughter had more tests and more ultrasounds, and all anyone could tell us was that the mass was very large and that they would know more once they began to remove it. They had an oncology team on standby, in case it was malignant. They were prepared for the worst. The doctor told us to go get something to eat and that he would be back to us in about four hours.

"Chinese food?" I asked my younger daughter, sister, and a few friends who had joined me at the hospital. We crammed into the elevator and emptied out onto First Avenue in search of lo mein. It was a cool but beautiful evening, and I felt bad for enjoying the feeling of the fresh air on my face. We sat at a big table in the window of the nearest Chinese place and small-talked about school and pets and things that had little connection to what was happening at the hospital a few blocks away. We all knew we were just there to pass time. When we couldn't drink any more tea and had run out of anything more to say to each other, we trekked back to the hospital's waiting room, leftovers in hand. That's where the surgeon found us six hours after the operation had begun—with empty take-out containers scattered around us like fallen heroes. He was smiling.

"She's fine and in recovery," he said. They were the most beautiful words I'd heard in a long time.

He told us he had removed an eighteen-pound tumor along with one ovary and a fallopian tube that had been completely enveloped by the mass.

He said he was able to get the tumor out in one piece, which was a massive feat—pun intended—as he didn't want any fluid from the tumor to leak into her abdominal cavity.

He said it was the largest tumor of its kind that he had ever removed.

He said that it took a little longer to get her to recovery because they had a group of residents come into the operating room to see him remove the mass in one piece.

He said they also had a photo session with the tumor and sent me a text of it on a surgical table with a dollar bill next to it for scale.

"Eighteen pounds," I repeated in complete shock. "That's bigger than the turkey I cooked for Thanksgiving."

How could we all have missed an eighteen-pound tumor? How could we not see it externally as it encircled and crowded her organs? How long had this thing been growing inside of her? What kind of a mother would fail to notice something like this? I chastised myself for not sensing that something was wrong with my daughter. Every time I told someone that she had an eighteen-pound tumor removed from her abdomen, I got the same response:

"How did it get so big before you discovered it?"

"You couldn't see it? There wasn't a lump or anything?"

"Wow. How long was it growing before you noticed something was wrong?"

"I had no idea," I said.

"It didn't show," I said.

"She was in pain, so we went to the ER," I said.

Rationally, it all made sense. There was no way I could have known, but emotionally I felt like I had let her down. I felt out of touch with my role as a mother and a caregiver to my children. I was so absorbed in my own issues—changes at work, unshakable sadness, dwindling confidence—that I missed an eighteen-pound tumor. *No one should miss an eighteen-pound tumor*, I thought. If someone told me this story about *their* daughter, I would have had all kinds of judgments about their parenting, awareness, and motherly love. For months after the extraction, I would punish myself (and everyone around me) with my embarrassment. "How are you doing?" someone might ask. "Well," I'd say, "my older daughter had a tumor removed from her abdomen that I never noticed. It was the size of a roasted turkey that could feed a family of ten with plenty for leftovers." No one stuck around to hear more.

On the day of her last appointment with her doctor—nine months after we first went to the ER—she was given an "all clear" and released from his follow-up care. The incision was healing fine, and there were no signs of malignancy.

"Go live your life" were the final words of advice from the surgeon. We got in the car and drove home.

"I'm moving to San Francisco," my daughter blurted out as I maneuvered the twists and turns of the parkway.

"What do you mean?" I asked.

"I mean I'm moving. The doctor said to go live my life, so that's what I'm going to do."

"Wait. I don't understand. When did you decide this? What's going on?"

"I've always wanted to go to San Francisco."

I wanted to pull over on the side of the road and look her in the face so she could explain to me when this cross-the-country plan was hatched and what she intended to do once she got there. I wanted to complain that I'd just nursed her back to health for nine months and that she couldn't just leave. I wanted to tell her that her sister was leaving for college soon and that I never thought she would leave New York—that she was "too New York" to leave. I needed to tell her that I was sorry that I missed the eighteen-pound tumor and that I would pay more attention from now on. I wanted to tell her not to leave me.

We didn't talk the rest of the way home. She said she had to start packing, book a ticket, and find a moving company. She had some appointments with realtors set up. I didn't understand why she had kept this a secret from me. I told her I felt betrayed.

"I knew you'd freak out, and I was right."

"Why would you say that?"

"Because that's what you do."

She laughed and shook her head when I told her how shocked I was that she saw me this way.

There's something that happens to my oldest child when she faces uncertainty in her life: she becomes very certain about certain things. It took her three days to pack up and move to San Francisco. She took her guitar with her and said she was going to find work as a musician.

"The tumor was a sign, Mom," she told me as we pulled into the driveway. "I need to go do things that make me happy."

It took me a moment to realize that what I was feeling was jealousy. I wanted—*needed*—a moment of realization like this. She was so sure. *I'd kill to feel this way*, I thought. At work I was making decisions all the time, but I never felt *sure* about any of them. I felt they were safe or logical or necessary or helpful but never completely without question. I wanted to feel so deeply and passionately that my own decisions were right and good. I wondered if there was a recent sign—a metaphorical tumor—that I had missed. Did I gloss over a moment of adversity that could have catapulted me toward big, passion-driven changes in my life? Would I get another chance? Would I recognize a sign or signal, even if it knocked me on the side of my head? Could I ever feel the kind of certainty my daughter now felt? I wished I had a tumor too, something that could be removed from me and change my life.

"I should have moved to Paris when I was about twenty-five," I blurted out to her as I walked into her bedroom after we got home from that final doctor visit where she'd been given a clean bill of health.

"Why?"

"Because I wanted to. It was a thought I had again and again about living there and being a writer. I wanted to have fun."

"So why didn't you?"

"I was scared," I told her. We stood looking at each other. I realized I was just as scared in that moment as I had ever been.

CHAPTER 3

SPRING 2013

"Well," I said at our morning staff meeting, "a year and a half ago *Ad Age* magazine called me an unlikely CEO when I was appointed to run this legendary advertising agency—you know, being female, promoted internally, first C-suite title for me—and they may have been right on paper. They also said I was up for fighting a good fight during our moment of crisis and, in this, they were absolutely right.

As I look at you, I see a team of unprecedented talent and determination, and I have no doubt that we will continue to break new ground in advertising. We have won business and we have lost business. We are at a critical turning point in the life of this agency, and we need to fight the good fight harder than ever now. Our situation should be looked at as both an opportunity and a catalyst. We're all in this together, as we have always been.

Most of you've been here long enough to remember that after one particularly grueling all-nighter, our presentation flew out the back window of the car while on the way to the meeting and littered Eighth Avenue with pages of ideas and designs—which I'm sure would have won us the business, if we actually presented the work, instead of losing it.

We've experienced some crazy times and have the stories to prove it! We traveled the globe to consult, create, and contribute our work and ideas to some of the world's most beloved and successful brands. If a company wanted to make style a substantive part of their identity, they called us. So what that we moved from the so-called penthouse to the ground floor! We're more than our surroundings and view. We're more than the decisions that were made for us. We're more than the cost-cutting that we had to go through.

Yes, we lost a lot of business—it's the nature of agency life. Yes, we have to save as many accounts as we can—and grow them. Let's remember who we are, what we have done, and what we know we're capable of doing. We have a lot to do in order to achieve our goal for growth, and I commit to doing everything in my power to stay focused on that goal. You know who you are, and I do too. Let's review what we've got going on. Remember, there are sharks in the water, circling."

We had just pitched and won a new piece of business that we needed to discuss. The job was to help a well-established brand develop new, innovative product ideas. We didn't get paid what we deserved, but we weren't in a position to walk away from the work. "We can nail this and then get more work from them," I said, "but first someone has to manage the client"—the one who'd called the account director and asked for more creative ideas than we had agreed to in our contract, before the ink had even dried. He wanted too much, and he knew it.

He knew we were operating a shifting business that couldn't afford to lose an assignment.

He knew we had some of the best talent in advertising working here.

He knew he could push us and get what he wanted.

He knew we needed to sacrifice our value to prove our worth again.

He knew we had to show quarterly improvements.

He knew we needed to rise like a phoenix from the ashes.

He knew he had us over a barrel.

I thought of the TV show *Mad Men* and what agency boss Roger Sterling said: "Being with a client is like being in a marriage. Sometimes you get into it for the wrong reasons, and eventually they hit you in the face."

"He's taking advantage of us," someone said.

"He's being a jerk," someone else said.

"I'll take him to lunch," I said.

I picked a restaurant that I thought would wow him, reassert our style, and give him confidence in the business. We had a good talk and came to an agreement as to how we would move forward in a way that was fair to both of us. I wasn't happy, but I knew we could make it work.

"Fake it till you make it. Again," I said to myself.

A few days later, he called the account director once again and asked for another round of creative ideas. This broke our lunch pact. I felt the inevitable slap, just like Roger predicted.

CHAPTER 4

LEVON HELM IS IN THE HOSPITAL

"Levon Helm is in the hospital," my mother called to tell me. It was the spring of 2012. She read it in the local paper. He was the drummer for The Band, the sixties group that backed Bob Dylan before they went on to record their own hits. The Band was famous for an album called "Music from Big Pink," released in 1968. "Big Pink" was the nickname for the pink-colored house they rented in West Saugerties, New York. I knew all this because I grew up in Saugerties. This was legendary stuff.

I took my daughter to see Levon play at his performance space in Woodstock, New York, about a year prior, while struggling to connect with her during my new, elevated role at work which was taking up much of my time, energy, and thoughts.

...while trying to prove to her that things were already changing for the better.

...while trying to show her that my new role was not an anchor.

...while trying to show her I'd still have time to do things with her.

We both loved listening to music from the sixties and frequently connected on this topic. *It's a perfect thing for us to do together,* I thought—an experience we can share and reminisce about, again and again. After we saw the concert, we entered true fandom. We started listening to music from The Band. We bought a photo of The Band by Norman Seeff and hung it on our kitchen wall so we could see it every day. We even decided to get away for a weekend and rented their old house, the one called Big Pink. I slept in the room that had been Garth Hudson's. My daughter slept in what we were told had been Levon's room. The night we went to the concert, one of the security people said that it was going to be a great show, that Levon's voice was good tonight. My daughter looked to me to translate. "He had throat cancer a few years ago," I said.

"What hospital?" I asked my mother, focusing back on the conversation at hand.

"The paper didn't say. It just said he's in the hospital in New York City."

"So sad," I said.

I told my daughter.

"I wish I could give him a get-well note," she said. I loved that her first reaction to hearing he was hospitalized was to help, to lift his spirits, and send him hope and love.

A light bulb flashed on in my head. *I can help with this*, I thought. *I can help her get a note to Levon. I can move my meetings to the afternoon, let her skip school, and accomplish this.* I could do something with my daughter that was uplifting for both of us.

"Why don't we try to find out which hospital he's in and drop your note off at the nurses' station. They'll get it to him."

"We don't know where he is."

"We can go around to the top cancer hospitals in the city and ask if he's there."

"Really? Is that OK to do? I can also mail it. He can get it when he's home."

"No. We have to try. It's kind and thoughtful and caring," I said a bit maniacally. "What have we got to lose except for a few hours of time?"

She wrote the note. I Googled "cancer hospitals nyc."

The first hospital we went to was Beth Israel. We walked in and told the guard at the desk that we had a delivery for Levon Helm. We showed him the handwritten envelope with the note inside. He checked the computer and told us he couldn't find a Levon Helm registered.

"Oh," I said. "Maybe we made a mistake. We might be at the wrong hospital. My mother told us he was here. Oh well. Thanks for your help."

"On to Mount Sinai," I directed.

We did the same thing. He wasn't there either.

Memorial Sloan Kettering was next on the list.

We walked in and went to the security desk.

"We have a delivery for Levon Helm. We want to leave it at the nurses' station."

The guard checked the computer.

He told us the floor and pointed toward the elevators.

My daughter grabbed my hand.

We did it. We found Levon, I thought to myself.

I thanked the guard, and we proceeded to the elevators. We wanted to drop off the note then leave, no hanging around. When the elevator door opened, we saw Levon's daughter and two of his band members standing across the hall. They were talking to a doctor. His daughter was crying.

"Let's go right to the nurses' station. We can't intrude," I said, not taking my eyes off the conversation that was unfolding right in front of us. It didn't occur to me that we were already intruding. It didn't cross my mind when we saw his daughter crying that we should have stayed in the elevator and gone back down to the lobby and out the front door. I wanted to deliver the note for my daughter. I was mission-driven for her, at the expense of propriety. The wrongness of this still felt good to me. I was at the helm of a well-known ad agency.

My decisions mattered, and I had decided to deliver this note come hell or high water.

"Let's go," I said to her.

"We have a note for Levon Helm," I told the woman at the counter, with all the officiousness I could exude.

"Oh," she said.

"Can we leave it with you to get to him, please?"

She looked blank. "Sure. You can leave it."

"Thank you!" I shouted forcefully.

We ran to the elevator like two children going out to play.

Outside the hospital, we stood on the street, stunned at what we'd just done. We had, through trial and error, found the hospital containing Levon Helm and dropped off a get-well note. I hoped he would read it and that he would write back to my daughter. *That would make her so happy*, I thought. I played out a scenario in my head where I got a call from the Helm family thanking me for our thoughtfulness and initiative. They wanted to hear the story of how we found him. They wanted to know all the details.

"It really lifted his spirits," they would say.

"It reminded him how loved he is by so many people."

"He was touched by the note."

"It made a difference."

I would tell them that it was nothing and that we were compelled by a higher force to get him the note. That it was almost like we were guided there. That we knew it was a weird thing to do, but we had no choice. It was destiny.

I learned a few days later that Levon Helm had died about fifteen minutes before we dropped off the note. It was in the paper. Now I knew what the family had been talking about in the hall with the doctor. I knew why the nurse looked at us expressionlessly. I scolded myself. *I should have known better*, I thought. We went to the obvious hospital choice last.

I told my daughter that Levon passed away and that our note arrived too late.

"Oh no," she sighed. "Do you think his family has it?"

"I'm sure it was given to his daughter. The nurses would never throw it out," I consoled.

Despite the outcome, I was elated. Delivering the note was an adventure, albeit a dark one. At first, I was worried that I stalked a dying man for my own salvation—that I stalked a dying man to impress my daughter with my can-do, never-give-up attitude. I knew that I was often straddling two worlds—moving among the living but trying to connect with the dead through frequent visits with mediums, psychics, and tarot card readers.

But this felt different. This felt hopeful.

"His funeral is next week, I said. "We should go to that."

We road-tripped to Woodstock. Levon's casket was on the stage in the barn, where he performed. It was next to his drum kit. My daughter and I waited in line to walk past his body and pay our respects. When we were in front of the stage, a drop of water seemed to come from nowhere and dripped down the side of the coffin.

"Look, Mom," she said.

"It's a tear," I told her. "Maybe he knows we tried to say goodbye." I looked up to see if there was a ceiling leak. There wasn't.

"People connect the way they can," I told her. "A breeze that ripples the curtains or sheets isn't always just a breeze."

"Maybe," she said.

I told my mother all about walking past the casket and seeing it cry a tear.

After a moment of silence, she quickly changed the topic, not wanting to discuss my otherworldly pursuits.

"You should have seen all the birds I had at the feeders this morning," she said, ending the conversation.

CHAPTER 5

GRANDPA, IS THAT YOU?

The stresses of work were causing me to lose a lot of sleep. There were nights when I felt like I tossed and turned constantly, getting very little rest. I was always tired and "a quart short" as my mother frequently noted. *I'm more than a quart short*, I thought. I was in over my head and drowning.

I woke early one morning before the sun was up, typical for me in my new sleepless state. But this morning was different. It felt like I was awoken by a touch to my foot. It was hanging off the bed, poking out from under the covers. I rolled over and opened my eyes. No one was there.

I knew my foot had been touched. It was as if someone was sitting at the foot of my bed, gently rubbing and jiggling my foot to wake me up. It was such a familiar feeling. My grandfather, who helped raise my sister and me, used to wake me this way every morning for school. I bolted upright in bed and let out the words "Grandpa, is that you?"

My heart was pounding. Ever since my beloved grandfather died in 1989, I had been longing for a vision or sign from him. One time I thought I saw his face in the clouds as I was lying in the grass, trying to connect with the universe in some way. I eventually thought I just imagined this or wished so hard to see him that I convinced myself I saw his face. It's like seeing the face of the man in the moon. It's not really there, but you can see it if you want to.

I looked around, waiting, sensing, and hoping he would manifest himself to me somehow. I thought I saw the curtains move out of the corner of my eye. I sank back into my pillow and stuck my foot out from under the covers, hoping he would come back.

I must have fallen asleep because when I woke, it was time to get up. I looked around my room. Everything was as it should have been. There was nothing left behind for me as proof of my grandfather's visit. I'm not sure what I was hoping to find—an odd button on the floor, an object out of place, a lingering scent—but I looked for anything. I wanted confirmation.

I told him how much I loved him and how I missed him every day. I cried for the loss of his actual touch and presence in my life. I wondered if I was going a little crazy, grasping for signs from above that would guide me. I worried about living in the past and counting on people for guidance that weren't in this world anymore. I prayed to all who loved me to guide me on my journey and to protect my children and me as we traveled forward in life. I wanted to believe so badly. I needed to believe in something outside of myself. I needed to believe my grandfather was there for me and that what I felt was not just a breeze rippling across the sheets.

"Good morning, Grandpa," I said aloud, to myself. "Thank you for waking me up. I miss you so much. I wish you were here. I really need you. My business is in trouble. My baby girl is leaving for college soon, and I'm about to be all alone. Nothing's good. Please help me."

I sat in bed and cried. I prayed he would see my pain and come back. I wanted him to grab my foot one more time and tell me to dry my eyes. I wanted to hear him say, "Hunker down," the way he always did when I needed to finish my homework or a chore or a project left undone. *If I feel his touch or presence again,* I told myself, *I'll hunker down. I'll get up, get dressed, and look on the bright side of things. I'll keep fighting the good fight. I won't feel so sorry for myself anymore. I'll imagine that there are great things to look forward to and that the business is on its way to becoming a thriving, successful enterprise, sought after by client after client. I'll happily anticipate preparing dinners and baking cookies or brownies when my children come to visit. I'll be thrilled to sit at the dining table for hours, just talking and catching up. I'll stop resenting them for growing up, for leaving home and living their lives. I'll quit being a downer to my little one about leaving for college.* I promised my grandfather that I would change and make things right for myself, if he would only send me one more sign.

He didn't come back.

I told my daughter about the visit from my grandfather and how I needed to be hyperconscious of anything that came into my periphery because I didn't want to miss him if he came to see me again.

"You know, Mom," she said, "some things are just what they seem. A curtain may have moved because of a draft."

"Yeah, I know," I said, not really believing this.

Around this time, I would often stare knowingly at the photo of Myrlie Evers—the widow of slain civil rights activist Medgar Evers—that hangs on a wall in my front hallway. It was taken at her husband's funeral. She has one tear streaming down her cheek. It was 1963 when Medgar was shot to death in front of his home. Fifty years later, Myrlie said she saw Medgar. He came into her kitchen wearing khaki pants and a blue shirt with the sleeves rolled up. He was, she said, "as large as life." Myrlie was sitting in a chair, and Medgar just walked by. When he passed her, he said, "I'm outta here." Myrlie was furious. He didn't even stop to look at her. She had to wait fifty years, and even then she didn't get what she wanted. Maybe I needed to be more patient.

I spent that morning running through lists of clients that were most likely to jump ship, trying not to think about my grandfather or the spot on my foot where I'd felt his touch. When I got back from picking up my lunch at the deli across Seventh Avenue, I had a message on my desk that one of our biggest clients called. We'd been through twenty-some rounds of creative development for an advertising campaign that seemed more like a moving target than a thoughtful assignment.

"Hey," I said, "how are you?"

He said he was great but had some "not happy" news to share. He got right to it. He was going to put the account up for review. It was time to look for a new ad agency. He said we could participate in the pitch and defend the business if we wanted. I asked him if we could re-pitch without a review. I asked him if we could be briefed on the business as if we were starting fresh. He said he wanted to see new thinking. I said we'd give him new thinking. I said I'd put a whole new team on it. He said he wanted to invite other agencies in to see their work. I said I'd invite other agencies in myself and that we could all work together—that I could tap into the best talent in our agency network. He asked how many clients we recently lost. "A few," I mumbled. After working for months on multitudes of creative development for him with not one advertising direction that looked like it was close to being approved, I *wanted* to say that we weren't going to participate. I *wanted* to tell the team that I would never put them through another round of work for a client that was having their own internal problems and growth pains. I wanted to stand in front of everyone and say, "Hey, if he didn't understand our work after seeing the largest and most brilliant range of creative solutions we have ever done for any client, then fuck him."

"Thank you," I said instead. "We look forward to seeing the new brief."

He wanted to terminate our contract as part of this process—a total fresh start if we kept the business and a quick goodbye if we didn't. "We have a sixty-day termination period," I reminded him. He asked if we could keep it to thirty days. I told him I'd run it by our CFO. I knew I was going to call him back with the "not happy" news that we were going to stick with the terms in the contract. After all, I had quarterly projections to submit soon, and a month would make a big difference. I sat down with our finance person to fill him in on my call. He asked what new business on the horizon was likely to close. I made a bad joke and said, "this business." He half-laughed. I regretted the comment. It wasn't appropriate. It lacked the seriousness, care, and concern that the question deserved.

"Let me check with the teams," I said, trying to recover my footing. "I'll get back to you tomorrow."

"We need to streamline things," I told everyone that afternoon, in a group meeting. My body was tense and joints stiff. I needed to be oiled, like the tin man in *The Wizard of Oz*. I wanted a new heart pumping fresh with fervor and passion and inspiration. I was beginning to feel hopeless. I could feel an oncoming despair in the deepening hunch of my shoulders.

"We're operating with a skeleton crew already," one of them said. "The copy machine is broken again, our printers can't handle the amount we're producing, and this morning, my desk collapsed. We're all coping, but there's nothing left to cut corners on or streamline."

"So true," I thought as I eyed his desk, now being held up by a filing cabinet instead of a leg.

"If we could do something—*anything*—differently to win new business while keeping the work we have, what would it be?" I asked.

After a moment of silence, the question was thrown back at me. Someone asked what my ideas were. *Nice punt*, I thought, *you'll do well wherever you work next.*

"I think we need a complete makeover. We need to totally reinvent our business offering, our value, and our approach. We need to relaunch this business. We need to be fast and smart and spend less to get more. We need to do for ourselves what we do for clients. We need to brand who we are and what we're good at. And tell the world. We'll activate all of our resources. We need to find what lifts us up, then use it to take off and fly. The sky's the limit," I said, feeling like I covered every cliché in the playbook.

I imagined a scene where we were all in a conference room with work—smart, incredible ad campaigns pinned to the walls surrounding us. We were batting around ideas, talking pros and cons of each direction. I saw myself sitting at the head of the table, fielding ideas from all the strategic and creative talent in the room—the best in the business. "Yes," I was saying, "this work is good; this work will change business for our clients and for us." I imagined that the coffee was flowing and fueling one great idea after another. I imagined there would be pizzas and salads, half-eaten on the side table, because we were on such a roll that we ordered in. We couldn't break for dinner because we were in the middle of reinventing the next new, new type of ad agency that would give our clients what they needed. The room would be electric with energy, hope, and optimism. No one would even think of going home until we cracked the nut and secured our future. We were laughing, because we felt good.

"But right now," I added, "we unfortunately need to clip our wings one more time. There will be some staff cuts coming based on business we've lost, which I'll discuss later today with the leadership team."

"Writing's on the wall?" someone asked somewhat humorously as the group mass exited the conference room.

I smiled and yelled into the cavernous silence that ended the meeting, "I hope not."

I could barely get it together to commute into the city every day for work.

It felt irresponsible.

It felt untrustworthy.

It felt exhausting.

It also felt oddly liberating not to care so much. After all, my older daughter was on the West Coast making music, my son was in Utah snowboarding and making movies, and my younger daughter was making herself ready to leave for college. I saw purpose and meaning slip away. The things I used to worry about were gone. I wondered what I was working so hard for anymore. It began to feel like I was scratching at an open wound when my job was to close up the incision and help it heal. I was struggling to rise to the occasion as much as the business was struggling to do the same. It was hard to muster up the enthusiasm and motivation to lead when I noticed that the number of people who showed up to work each day began to decrease. But who could blame them? They had wives, husbands, partners, children, and lives to support. They had dreams and desires. They had bills to pay, worries to assuage, and careers to grow. There wasn't a day since I'd taken the job when the entire team was in the office at one time. *They have their own stuff to take care of*, I thought.

"You know he's at an interview," I was quietly told by someone when I walked through the office and dropped a piece of paper on a vacant desk chair.

"I know," I said. "We talked about it. He's looking. Anyone else?"

"Everyone. Everyone is just looking to see what else is out there… to have a plan B."

"I understand," I said.

"These are uncertain times."

"What did you do last night?" I asked, wanting to change the subject.

"I worked on my résumé."

I couldn't shake the feeling that the team was coming to work only until they found something more certain, and I couldn't blame them. Life at the office had become nothing more than a series of nos to everyday questions and requests that should have been easy yesses.

"No, we can't hire anyone right now."

"No, there are no bonuses this year."

"No, that chair will have to do."

"No, we can't spend any more."

"No, that costs too much."

"No. I'm sorry."

"No. We can't right now."

"No."

"Um...no."

"No."

I looked at my schedule and planned a few days off, which seemed the opposite of what I should be doing, but I needed time to think, away from the problems and predicaments at work. Someone at the office said that if I was afraid to take a few days off because I was so worried things would tank, then we should just hang it up now.

"No," I said, "that's a good point."

I saw a quote from Rumi on Pinterest. It said, "Live life as if everything is rigged in your favor." *Yes*, I said to myself. *I need to look on the bright side a little more.*

But nothing seemed as if it was leading me down a path toward my ultimate benefit. Spending time with my daughter as she was finishing up her senior year and making plans for college in the fall was becoming its own problem. I wanted to be happy for her, but I was too unhappy for myself. Every trip to the grocery store had an element of finality to it: *This could be the last time we food shop together.* The movie we watched over the weekend: *This could be the last time we laugh and eat popcorn together.* A drive to the city: *This is ending soon.* I wanted to turn back the clock to when things seemed better, easier and less desperate.

"Remember the nineties?" I asked wistfully during a morning staff meeting.

"Remember when clients and agencies both had budgets? I heard a story about a client who was told that the photo shoot for their new ad campaign needed to happen in Paris, France, because Paris was the City of Light. The entire shoot was done indoors, in a lit photo studio. It could have been in any studio, anywhere in the world. No one cared. There was money to burn. You could easily win business from big agencies by being more creative, or more integrated, or more of anything they weren't. The internet was new. It was alternative! Those days are gone. Nothing's the same. Nothing's as straightforward or easy as it used to be. This is new territory, and our resources are slimmer than ever. I'm driving in tomorrow with some chairs from my house so we can set up an area in the office for a photo shoot. We need a good portrait of the leadership team. One of the account people has a camera we can borrow. And one of the creatives is going to be the photographer. We can retouch it in house. Wear all black. Let's look serious. Like we mean business."

"Why are you bringing in chairs from home?" someone asked.

"Because we need some variety," I said. "I don't want us all sitting on knock-off Knoll furniture."

"Let's take a few shots, please," said one of the creative directors, laughing. I want to be able to Photoshop the best pictures of my head and body together."

I wondered if we, too, were just Frankensteining ourselves back to life.

An email popped up in my inbox while I was sitting at home after a day at work, catching up on *The Real Housewives*. It was from our biggest client. They wanted to know if I could meet them in the morning for breakfast. I knew what this was going to be about. You can always tell when clients are about to fire you. They cancel meetings. They postpone work and push due dates forward, saying things like, "We want to re-brief you, so don't spend any more time on this." They don't return phone calls as quickly as they used to. Their tone changes. Less chatty. More serious. Slightly nervous. All business. And they email you at night asking for breakfast early the next morning.

"No problem," I emailed back. "Let me know when and where."

I sent a note to my team to tell them what was happening and that I'd be in the office after this meeting.

"Do you know what it's about?" someone replied to the email.

"I can probably guess," I wrote, knowing our key client contact was on the way out of the job and that when someone new on the client side comes in, making a change in the ad agency is almost inevitable.

This was the second client that was undergoing their own internal upheaval. It was like the perfect storm. I felt deadly forces from all directions merging to create singular, unparalleled turbulence.

The office was quiet when I arrived late morning. Everyone was waiting for me to get back from the breakfast meeting. I walked in and made eye contact with our head of strategy. I signaled him to follow me into my office.

"You want the door closed, I assume," he said.

"Yes."

"You don't look happy."

"I don't have good news. The account is being put up for review. We can defend it, if we choose. This is the second big piece of business we could lose within a matter of months. Without both of them, we don't have enough monthly income to keep the lights on. Basically, our future for the next several months could look like this:

We agree to work on the two big pitches and try to keep our top two accounts. The teams really need to bring new thinking, which I have no doubt will happen.

We work on getting new business to replace them, in case we lose. Keeping these clients is a long shot—we have new direct reports who obviously want to bring in their own team and make their own mark. We're being allowed to defend the accounts as a courtesy, which means we better come up with something undeniably good. This is the feeling I have from both clients. If we succeed in replacing these two pieces of business at the same revenue levels, this will bring us back to zero.

At the same time, we need teams working on getting additional business so we can grow.

We can't hire more help. We can't support our talent.

There aren't enough hours in the day, cups of coffee, stale conference room bagels, or ropes long enough to pull us up and put us back on top." I stopped when I heard myself digressing. I noticed that my strategic plan forward had quickly devolved into hopelessness and resignation. His concerned expression brought me back to the reality of the situation.

It was finally all becoming clear to me. I was walking the walk at the office. I was talking the talk of *we're in this together; let's get this done; we can do it; we've done it before*, interspersed with team lunches and popping open bottles of wine at 5:00 p.m. that weren't replacements for a shifting industry and business exodus. They were just vestiges of another time—facades of fun and frivolity that I had no business assuming anymore.

I could not fix things.

"I know we're so close to winning a bunch of new business," I started again, "yet we're so far. There are no contracts out for signature. We're still in the talking phase, and you know how long it usually takes to move past that. We're the ones under pressure, not the clients. We can't force them to meet our timeline. They just won't. And I feel like a bottom-feeder. We're picking up accounts we wouldn't have even considered not that long ago. But beggars can't be choosers. Also, my daughter is leaving for college in a few months. I'm a mess; there, I said it. This has been harder than I ever thought it would be. The thought of her leaving, of me in the house, all alone. I can't have another lunch or drinks meeting or dinner that goes nowhere. I'm getting fucking huge. My clothes don't fit right. There's always a button I can't close. I can show you. My pants are open now. I've thrown out half my clothes in depression-driven fits. It's called 'rage cleaning.' Listen, when you go out at the top—before the walls come crumbling down or some young, two-person team that split from a big agency to open their own shop pulls away all your business for a quarter of the amount—you're always the champ, right? We still have our reputations intact, and our self-esteem hasn't been dredged out of us yet, right?"

I wondered if I was the only one who didn't see this coming.

I wondered if the decision to elevate me to CEO felt as weird to them as to industry commenters.

I wondered when they realized that I wasn't the bright and shiny face of a new beginning.

"I'm sorry to dump this on you," I continued. "I've been doing a lot of thinking—those days off really helped me solidify my thoughts— and I've come to a decision, which makes sense after today's meeting. I think the brave thing to do is not hold on by our teeth. We need to recognize the difficulties we face. I don't want to spew false hope or worse, have my head in the sand. We all have families to support and careers to nurture. Sometimes the best path forward is to just stop."

The next day was, mercifully, Saturday. I couldn't wait to stay in bed late into the morning and weep, calling for my dead grandfather to help. I longed to tuck under the covers and hide—disappear from what my life had become. What would my grandfather want me to do now? I was entering a downward spiral. I couldn't see anything in my life that was going the way I wanted it to go. I lay there waiting for the curtains to move or an ethereal breeze to ripple the sheets. If I felt any pressure to do something, to be productive, it was to make him proud. In death as in life. *He would want me to work harder,* I thought. He worked hard all his life. He would want me to have friends and be happy. He would want me to take care of myself and be healthy. He always attributed "clean living" to his successes. *I was too dirty for him,* I thought. *This is why he doesn't give me a sign that he's here for me.* My life was filthy with compromise, self-loathing, and pity. I knew that he would hate to see me this way, as a failure. I apologized to him and rolled over, becoming invisible under the covers.

I enveloped myself in a shroud of sheets and thought about the day he died. I was pregnant with my first child. I had recorded her heartbeat when I went to the obstetrician for a check-up. I wanted him to hear his great-granddaughter, to meet her. I took the recording to him. He was in the hospital, folded into his own sheets like something already half-disappeared. He cried and nodded at me as he listened to the heartbeat. "Yes, this is good," he seemed to say. He stopped breathing shortly after that. I was holding his hand when he passed. His eyes were open, and it seemed like he was looking at something. I hoped his parents were waving to him to come join them. I pulled back my own sheets that were now wet with my tears, sat up, and screamed:

"Grandpa, I need you!"

CHAPTER 6

THE CAUTIONARY TAIL

I couldn't shake the feeling that I was being irresponsible, negligent, aloof, and that I could have cared with more intensity and acted with more urgency. I was letting my life get away from me and couldn't muster up the energy to take charge. I remembered this feeling well. It was familiar to me. It nagged at me. I had a habit of being so emotionally distant in order to keep it together and not burst into tears at a moment's notice, that I was actually out of touch. *This is why my cat died*, I remembered. *Or no*, I finally admitted to myself, *this is how I killed my cat, Cooper*.

I found my cat's tail in the middle of the driveway. The rest of the cat was missing.

I took the bloody stump and wrapped it in aluminum foil. Cooper was an outdoor cat so I thought I might find her hiding somewhere in the yard, near the barn where she lived. Scared. Tailless. *Maybe it can be reconnected*, I thought. I put the tail in the refrigerator—in the back, so my daughter wouldn't see it and pull it out of the fridge, thinking it was a snack.

I walked around the yard calling for Cooper. He was a calico we'd gotten from a farm in upstate New York. The farm was next to the cemetery where my grandfather was buried. I imagined that the soil connected them somehow. I knew that was really a stretch, a wild excuse. I just wanted a cat and wouldn't let myself admit it. I didn't think I deserved to have something else that needed my care. Turned out I was right. The cat was missing and the severed tail was found in the driveway. I searched for her until my daughter came home from school.

"I have to tell you something," I said.

"What?"

"Cooper is missing."

"How do you know? Maybe she's just hiding somewhere."

"No. I think something happened."

"Why? You're scaring me."

"I have her tail in the refrigerator. I found it in the driveway."

"Let me see it," she said.

I opened the foil to reveal it to her. Tears flowed. *She's probably dead*, I worried.

I told my daughter there was hope and that we might find her. We went outside and searched the perimeter of the house, moving in opposite directions. There was no sign of her. I was glad that we didn't find her body lying in the lawn or at the edge of the woods that surrounded the house. I didn't know what I'd do. I had a shovel with me to scoop her up if we found her, but then what?

I reminded my daughter where the tail was in the refrigerator and told her not to open it up. I told her I'd keep it there for bit, just in case.

"We have Cooper's tail, so we actually still have a cat," I told her optimistically.

She cried and went to her room. I scolded myself for trying to console my daughter on the loss of her cat by pointing out that the wrapped-up bloody tail was a stand-in for our pet.

"Sorry," I called out after her. She didn't respond.

I had made the cat live outside, in the barn, because that was the most I could manage. And now all I had left was another reminder that I was negligent, dangerously careless. I couldn't trust myself.

Three days later, however, Cooper miraculously walked into the driveway like nothing had happened, like she didn't have a gaping hole in her backside. *Three days*, I thought. She was resurrected. *She was from sacred soil*, I reminded myself. I grabbed the tail from the refrigerator, placed the cat into her carrier, and drove directly to the animal hospital. "You won't believe what happened," I said to the vet as I handed him the wrapped-up tail.

"It's not like a finger," he said. "We'll dispose of it for you, if that's OK."

"Sure," I said. I was happy to get it out of the house.

"She's been missing for three days," I told the vet.

"She looks good. She's going to be fine, albeit tailless."

"Three days," I repeated. I wanted him to pick up on the significance of this. I wanted him to recognize the possibility of resurrection.

"It's weird," he said, ignoring my vague hints. "I don't see any marks on her that would tell us how the tail got pulled off. The wound is clean. It's like it just fell off her body."

"Weird." I nodded. I caught myself lost in thought, pondering the idea of the cat being resurrected and having something do to with my grandfather's spirit—something to do with a sharing of soil. I was fairly sure that this was a sign. It was more than a breeze or the ruffle of curtains. *It had to be a message*, I thought. I knew I needed to keep this to myself. I imagined any conversation on the topic of Cooper's resurrection would not be received well by my daughter or anyone else. On one hand, I knew this was an out-there, crazy thought. The cat was injured by someone or something and was hurt and hiding for three days until she found her way home. On the other hand, I was desperate and needed the possibility that greater forces had been involved. I couldn't (or wouldn't) shake the feeling that a miracle had happened. It gave me chills. It gave me hope.

Cooper went back to the barn. I still didn't bring her into the house, even after all she'd gone through. I locked her in the barn at dusk. It was safer than being outside at night. I felt like I was finally being responsible. I felt like I had figured it out. But in reality, I had a tailless cat locked in my barn at night because I couldn't bring myself to relocate her to the house.

"Move her into the house," my sister said.

"She's an outdoor cat," I emphasized. I didn't tell her about the three days, the sacred soil, or that I was actually scared of having a cat that had come back from the dead walking around my house.

"She's injured. She needs love."

"I know how she feels."

"Your tail wasn't found in the driveway."

"No, but it's between my legs. I'll bring her inside," I lied.

Soon after this, Cooper got out of the barn one night, and we never saw her again.

CHAPTER 7

GOODBYE TO ALL THIS

When the news broke that my role as CEO was coming to an end and the ad agency was closing, I was out of the office with my daughter, visiting the college that she would be attending. We were tromping through buildings and classrooms and a wide-open field at the edge of a Vermont campus known to students as the End of the World. The agency receptionist emailed me that a reporter was buzzing the front door, asking to come in and speak with me.

"Did you open the door?" I asked.

"Yes."

"What did they want?"

"He said he left you several messages but you never called back." This was true.

"What did you say?"

"I said you weren't here, and he said to please get you the message if you wanted to be included in the story."

"Did he say what story?"

"No. He wanted to walk around, but I wouldn't let him, obviously, so he left."

I wished I could have called back right away and told him things were great—amazing, actually. I wanted to say that we were doubling our growth over the upcoming year, clients were thrilled, and we were fielding new business calls on a daily basis. I wanted to say, "How nice of you to check in on us" and "I can't wait to see the story on our success." But I knew none of these scenarios were even close to reality, so I avoided calling back.

When I got home the next day, I returned the reporter's call before I went into the office. I silently lamented that, with all our experience and talent, we couldn't win enough new business, fast enough, to lift the advertising agency out of its slump. The reorganization that resulted in thrusting me to the position of CEO wasn't helping, and even creating our own marketing campaign to give away a free strategy session over a free breakfast as a way to entice new business did not produce one single taker. The reporter picked up my call.

"Yes," I said, "the business is closing soon."

"Yes," I said, "everyone here knows and people are already looking for new jobs and, in fact, many have already taken new positions elsewhere."

"Yes," I said, "clients are being transitioned to other agencies within our network."

"No," I said, "it was a personal decision to close the agency."

"No," I said, "ownership is behind me all the way."

"No," I said, "I was not pressured by management."

"Yes," I said, "it is one of the saddest days of my life."

There is a parable in the form of a joke about a man stranded on the roof of his home during a flood, praying to God to be rescued. As he was praying, a person in a rowboat passed by and told him to jump in. The man said, "No," that he was waiting for God. A few minutes later, a motorboat came by and the passengers told the man to come aboard. "No," he said. God was coming for him. Next, a helicopter flying above dropped a rope down for him. The man waved it off, hollering that God was on the way. The water kept rising, and the man on the roof drowned and went to heaven. When he got to the Pearly Gates and met God, he said, "God, I prayed to you for rescue, and you let me down." God replied, "I sent you a rowboat, a motorboat, and a helicopter. What more did you expect?" I wanted to complain to God too. I wanted to let God know that I really tried, that I was sincere and hardworking in my efforts. I wanted it known that I recognized help and never once refused it. I wanted to say that I never intended to drown and that I wasn't like the man on the roof, even though I felt like it. I wondered if there was a rope that I'd failed to grab.

I walked into the office that afternoon, back from the college visit with my daughter, thinking I just went from one End of the World to another. My heart was pounding. I closed the door behind me then decided that didn't look right and left it a crack opened—just enough for the few people who were still coming to work to know I was inside but not enough to seem like anyone could just walk in. I felt like hiding.

I started to move unpacked items around my desk, putting them into neat piles, for no particular reason. There were notebooks, filled with meeting notes, to-do lists, thoughts, and ideas. I contemplated their value. What if there was something in them that I might need someday? They contained shadows of a past that was not coming back. The notes were ghosts, left over from another life—a life I was about to pack up and pack in. Yet I was afraid to throw things out. What if I needed a file, a presentation? What if there was a phone number scribbled in the margin of a pad that I would never be able to get again if I threw everything out? It was too final a moment for me. I decided to box everything up and take it all with me. I couldn't throw away my work life.

I checked my email. Nothing new had come in since I left on my ninety-minute commute to the office. The bare white walls glared at me. "Light's out," they seemed to say. I was squinting at the sun shining through the window, pushing back the tears. I pulled a small mirror from my bag to check my face for signs of life. I looked one hundred years old. Crow's feet were etched deep into my face like dry river beds. My complexion was sallow and my skin so thin that I could see veins protruding—pulsing—as unwelcomed reminders of stress. My cheeks had no color. My hair was falling out. My long hair, that I unfortunately received more positive comments about than my new role as CEO when my photo appeared in a business story, was shedding onto my slumped shoulders. I wiped my eyes and slammed the mirror shut.

As I walked into the large open studio area in the office, people were working as usual. *It looks so normal*, I thought and wondered if this was what it felt like right before a disaster: people just going about their life and business until they're wrenched out of it by unseen forces beyond their control—just listening to music, talking on the phone, or thinking about what to have for lunch—until the bomb explodes.

Until body parts are torn from their sockets.

Until blood stains the carpet.

Until destruction rips a gaping hole to the outside world.

I shuddered at my own doomsday thoughts and images.

"Hey," I said to everyone, trying to reimagine a happier scene as I looked into all their faces.

One person asked me how the college visit went. Another asked me if I wanted to meet in a bit to look at some final client deliverables. The office manager asked if we should order more boxes for packing, and one of the executive creative directors asked if he could have the coffee maker.

"Yes, take the coffee maker. Take the coffee too."

"Well, that's it for me," someone joked. "I can't work without coffee."

"Neither can I," I added.

When the business shut down, I entered a surreal and unsustainable limbo. Life at home, without the pressures and the structure of the ad agency, was nothing but a sequence of good days (which were bad days) and bad days (which were horrible).

On a good day, I'd cut my hair over the bathroom sink and regret it. *It will grow back*, I'd remind myself.

On a bad day, I wouldn't get out of bed. I'd watch Bravo all day.

On a good day, I'd journal and get my feelings out. It felt like progress, except for all the sobbing.

On a bad day, I'd rip through my closet, bagging up all my clothes that didn't fit anymore. I'd take them to Goodwill.

On a good day, I'd look in my closet for a shirt that I wanted to wear and realize I threw it out. I'd buy a new one.

On a bad day, I'd go to the local hardware store and buy work clothes. I felt that if I looked like I had just finished doing some yard work, my slovenly demeanor would be excused.

On a good day, I'd check my email and send responses as needed, the phrase "The End of the World" running through my head.

On a bad day, I'd delete emails without reading them.

On a good day, I'd shop for things with my daughter that she needed for her dorm room and have a great time...until I remembered she was leaving me soon.

On a bad day, I'd tell her I'd rather not discuss college stuff and ask her to close my door on her way out.

On a good day, I'd drink a bottle of wine and pass out.

On a bad day, the specter of my daughter waving goodbye in the rearview mirror as I drove away from taking her to college would play over and over in my mind, like a premonition from a horror movie.

I don't know why I thought that I might be able have it all, do it all. I never really believed anyone could. I had never once seen it happen to anyone. Something always had to give, and that something was different for each of us. In my case, I didn't think the thing that gave way would be my self-esteem. I didn't think it would be my career. I didn't think it would be *me*. I thought it would be something pettier, like downsizing my home after all the kids were gone or taking a long vacation and leaving the business in my partner's hands for a month while I soul-searched. I didn't know that the thing that would *give* would be my entire sense of self, my whole reason for living.

End of the World, I kept thinking.

CHAPTER 8

LISTEN TO THE MUSIC PLAY

"What's Furthur?" I asked my teenage daughter when she told me she wanted to see them. She said they're basically the Grateful Dead minus Jerry Garcia. "Right," I said, "because he's dead." I was secretly relieved that we would never have to make plans to attend his funeral or memorial service like we did for Levon. She said they were playing a nine-show residency, only about thirty minutes from our house. She said we could go to all the shows if I wanted to because they would play a different set every night. She said that I didn't have to get up for work anymore, so maybe it would be good for me to go out—to stay awake past 9:00, which was becoming my default bedtime. She said it would be fun.

I couldn't decide if she was being opportunistic, trying to cheer me up, or attempting to keep me awake and alive in the world around me. Nonetheless, it felt good to be asked by her do to something together. It felt good to be able to say yes to her. I had no idea what to expect but was looking forward to it.

"I think I'll be good for two or three nights, max," I negotiated.

I wanted to make her happy and, in doing so, thought I could feel some of this happiness as well. I forgot what having fun felt like. It

43

wasn't just that I wasn't always in the best mood; it was that I hadn't been able to show my better self to the people who needed me for far too long. My mind had drifted away from my daughter and her needs to settle on *my* needs, *my* problems. I knew this multi-concert caravan would be good for us.

I noticed a few things right away while at our first show. The audience cared about the order of the songs. It meant something to them. They cared about hearing set lists that were unique in terms of the songs played and the order they were played in. They reminisced about other great set lists. On the way out, they said things to each other like:

"Can you believe that 'Truckin'' was followed by 'Bertha'?"

"What was the encore?" someone asked as we walked out one night.

Where was he, and how did he miss this, I thought.

"'Attics of My Life,'" my daughter called out.

I joined in on the set list mania after the first concert.

"That was an unexpected encore," I would say to whoever was in earshot.

"I haven't heard a set begin with that song in a long time," I would ruminate aloud. I had no idea what I was talking about. I felt unchained.

I noticed that there was a regular group of followers that knew each other and discussed how they got to the show, where they were staying, and what other shows they were going to. Everyone knew the guy who sold tie-dyed socks, because he also sold tabs of acid. The Wharf Rats were the sober Deadheads. They made a prayer circle during set breaks and ate candy throughout the show. They talked about the bass player, Phil Lesh, and how at the end of every show he made a "liver speech." It was apparently known to fans as Phil's donor rap. He talked about the liver transplant that saved his life. He advocated for organ donation. I looked around, not sure this was the right crowd for a plea like this.

This was an easy world to live in. It required nothing of me. It was like traveling to a foreign land where no one knew your past and no one cared to ask about it. No one asked what I thought of the ad campaign that had just launched. No one cared about brand strategy. No one wanted my opinion on a logo, a tagline, or an advertising idea.

No one shook their head from side to side and said, "Sorry to hear what happened; it sounds like you tried your best."

No one gave me an elbow nudge and asked whether I was going to open my own advertising agency.

And thankfully, no one asked me how I was doing, which was a question I could only answer by bursting into tears.

CHAPTER 9

THE GIMP IS BACK

"I just feel so bad about myself," I cried. "I've always worked. I've had a job since I was fifteen years old. I've worked through ups and downs, and nothing has stopped me. Until now. You know when you're wearing high heels and one of them gets caught in a crack and you try to keep walking, but one heel is stuck and you can't move? That's how I feel. I can't move forward. But instead of freeing the heel, I imagine leaving it behind, sticking out of the crack in mid-step. I watch myself limp along, with just one shoe."

"I'm sorry, Mama," my daughter consoled.

"I mean, I just sit around in your brother's sweatpants from high school that I took from his closet and do nothing to help myself. I worry about being seen as diminished, less than I want to be. I'm ashamed and limping and missing a shoe. That's how I see myself. That's how I'm sure everyone sees me too. Old, ugly, worthless."

"I think you're beautiful."

"You have to say that."

"No, it's true, and until you see that, you're never going to get back in the world. You're focusing on the wrong things. You didn't learn anything from those concerts. You're obsessed with this idea of youth."

"I am not." I scowled, knowing she was referring to my regular Botox treatments, hair-coloring appointments, and strict anti-wrinkle skincare regimen. "I'm obsessed with feeling better, with feeling like I can get out of bed and not collapse on the floor of my closet because my pants won't close. I'm obsessed with finding the energy I need to do something productive. I'm obsessed with trying to figure out my life—to have a life. I don't even have a friend I can call for a coffee. I bump into people I know at the coffee shop who say, 'Sit down, join us.' All my encounters are by chance. I'm an accidental socializer. I can't make anything happen on my own anymore. Everything happens to me, and that's a problem because I never know if it's going to be a good or bad encounter, so I just get up, put on my sweats, and hope for the best. I go out for facials and massages and beauty appointments that I call 'self-care' but am well aware they are self-indulgent time killers. I'm not completely deluded about what I'm doing. I just can't help it right now."

I need to stop unraveling in front of her, I thought.

"Remember when you were a little girl and I hurt my hip somehow?" I continued. "It was hard to walk and everyone called me the Gimp? I'm the Gimp again." I shrugged my shoulders. "I guess it could be worse," I said. And thus ended my sad monologue.

"I'm going to make you a PowerPoint," my daughter said.

She knows me, I thought.

"Really? What's it about?"

"You."

"Email it to me. That's how I work," I said, trying to make it sound like a joke when we both knew I wasn't joking. I wasn't sure what to expect and wanted to see it alone. My emotions were unreliable.

"I'll just show you on my computer."

"Just email me. I want to read it alone. You're making me nervous."

My daughter walked to her bedroom across the hall from mine. It didn't take her very long to send me the email. The subject was a smiley face. I smiled back.

Page one was Gertrude Stein. Page two, Gloria Steinem. Page three, George Eliot. Page four, Lydia Davis. Page five, Yoko Ono. Pages six through ten, silver-haired models over the age of fifty from ads and magazine editorials. Captions read, "smart," "natural," "beautiful," and other words and thoughts adhering to this group of talented, successful women that derived value from what they did and who they were and not necessarily from what they looked like.

I called her in her bedroom, on her cell phone.

"Are you kidding me? How do you know that Lydia Davis isn't dying to get Botox? You're comparing me to George Eliot?"

"I want you to see how natural and beautiful all these women we love are. Like you."

"I do not look anything like Gertrude Stein. By the way, I haven't given up yet, although it seems like you think I have."

I told her I didn't appreciate the PowerPoint. I called her a jerk and hung up.

I walked to her bedroom to apologize. It was actually nice of her to help. *Maybe she's right*, I thought. I needed to focus on what's inside and worry less about my outward appearance. *But no, the PowerPoint was not helpful.* It was easy for a teenager to have this point of view. She didn't get it. Or maybe both things were true? She was right: I was misguided and self-pitying; she was wrong: I had to live in the real world where appearances mattered and you were judged constantly. I stopped myself from knocking on her door.

"I'm going to sleep," I yelled from the hallway, "so don't come in."

I gimped back to bed. I was less than I wanted to be for her. I wanted to help her make her dreams come true. I wanted us to spend time together, go on adventures, solve problems, make our world a safe and happy place. But I was the Gimp again, and all the Gimp could do was limp lazily from one room to another and think about the day her daughter would be leaving for college, which was circled on the calendar hanging on the back of her door, a portal to her and a bottomless pit to me.

End of the World.

YOU LOOK LIKE JONI MITCHELL

The calendar had no respect for my decision to ignore it and pretend that time wasn't marching on. It was July, and that meant that it would soon be September and then I'd be alone. *It's time to rise to the occasion, put my self-pity on a shelf, and have one final, amazing moment together before she leaves for school. Like the good ole days,* I thought, thinking of our time seeing Levon in concert. Thinking of our multiple nights with Furthur. Thinking of all the music we'd listened to that became the soundtrack of our relationship and time spent together. It was the least I could do. It was most I could do.

Canandaigua, New York, was a five-hour car ride away. We left from home in the morning so we could get there early and hang out before the show. Furthur was on their summer 2013 tour, and this would be our last concert before my daughter had to leave for college. I packed a jar of peanut butter and a loaf of bread, a six-pack of bottled water, bug spray, hand sanitizer, and a blanket to sit on.

"Don't forget cash," my daughter said. "You know there's always someone making a good grilled cheese out of the trunk of their car."

This is what a road trip should feel like, I thought. My daughter was more friend than child. It felt good to be thinking about doing something together instead of thinking about how soon she would move out. I liked being together, and I liked not thinking about being apart. We made sandwiches on the dashboard and ate Combos and Cheez-Its from gas station convenience stores. I said yes to a detour that promised a more interesting route than a highway. I said yes to turning up the radio. I said yes to driving with the windows down. It felt good not saying no, which was my short, but complete, sentence of choice these days.

We parked in a lot, and I noted our proximity to a large pine tree so that we could find the car in the dark when the concert was over. We walked to the vendor area, which was called Shakedown Street. It was full of people selling food, clothes, accessories, and everything and anything Grateful Dead. My daughter bought a handprint that was burned into an oval piece of wood. The hand was missing a finger.

"Why would you buy that?" I questioned.

"It's Jerry Garcia's handprint."

"He's missing a finger?"

"Yeah, where have you been?"

I had no idea that he'd had four and a quarter fingers on one hand. *Why would I*, I thought, *I never saw him play*.

A man hooked up to an oxygen tank that he pulled behind him in a red wagon was selling cookies.

"Buy some cookies?"

"What kind?"

"Oatmeal."

He said he only had one container left and that he was twenty-five dollars short of the money he needed to buy a bus ticket to Seattle to go live with his daughter.

I gave him the money he wanted and took the cookies.

"Are you sure they're not weed cookies?" my daughter asked.

"I don't think so. He didn't mention that."

"Don't eat too many," she warned. "Just in case."

They smelled good.

51

We split up at this point. I didn't want to stand in the front, at the stage. I wanted to sit in the back and eat my cookies. The field was full of cow pies. I kicked some shit out of the way and put my blanket on the ground. The cookies were good. I ate three. They weren't that big.

The couple to the left of me stripped naked and lay down next to each other on their blanket. I tried not to stare but couldn't help it. They were flat on their backs and motionless. Their arms were by their sides, palms up. I guessed that they were soaking in the vibes.

The man with the oxygen tank came back selling more cookies. He told me the same story and asked for another twenty-five dollars. He didn't seem to notice I was eating his cookies from the container he already sold me. I said no thanks, figuring I'd already done my community service. He moved on.

I tried to use the porta-potty, but it was too disgusting. My daughter warned me about this obstacle. I took the napkins she made me stuff into my pocket and walked into the brush next to the field to relieve myself. I wasn't alone.

Someone was sitting on my blanket when I got back from peeing. "Hi," I said. "This is my blanket." He said he thought it was abandoned. "It's not," I said and asked him to get up. He looked at me for what seemed like ten minutes before he stood. He asked to sit on a corner of it, but I told him I was waiting for someone. He nodded and noted that it was a big blanket as he walked away.

"Cool," I said.

The couple to the right of me reached over and handed me a joint.

"No thanks," I said.

I offered them a cookie in return. They declined when I confirmed they were not weed cookies.

The girl smiled at me. "It's finally kicking in."

"Cool," I said. Again.

I wore a hat that night. I never wore hats. It was a floppy crocheted black beret that had been in my drawer for years—a regretted purchase whose time to shine had finally come. It felt like it was the right time and place to wear a hat. This hat. It tipped to one side of my head. I liked being out of my comfort zone at these concerts. I was an old hippie here with a lot of other old hippies, and it made me feel free. *I would never wear this hat at home,* I thought. I also thought that if I ever saw anyone else wearing this hat, I would laugh. The hat was ridiculous.

The band played a song that made everyone stand up and dance. I joined in. A man walked over next to me. "You look like Joni Mitchell," he said.

I offered him a cookie.

He asked me if they were weed cookies. "No thanks," he said when I told him they were not. He said that he was really high anyway. He asked if he could kiss me.

"No," I laughed. He tried to dance with me, but I gave him no energy, and he eventually wandered away. I immediately missed him and wished I had been nicer. I liked the way the attention made me feel. It wasn't much, but it was enough. I felt attractive. I didn't feel like me. I looked around for him. *I would let him sit on my blanket if he wandered back over. I might even kiss him*, I thought.

I met my daughter at the porta-potties when the concert was over. A man selling balloons filled with nitrous oxide passed us. "Ten dollars a balloon," he called out to the exiting crowd. "Get your hippie crack."

"They call them the nitrous mafia," my daughter whispered.

We watched a woman inhale a balloon then pass out and hit her head on the curb. She didn't move. The people she was with ran over to help her. They pulled her up to a seated position and tended to her bleeding scalp.

"Wow," I said. "That was scary."

"Yeah," my daughter said, "I don't like the balloons."

I decided to let this go. *Don't question her*, I told myself. She was next to me. We were together. It was all I needed to care about at this moment. She was leaving for college in seven weeks. I knew my next and last road trip with her would be to take her to school. I would be driving home alone. I would be living alone. I would be all alone. I wondered if anyone else would tell me I looked like Joni Mitchell if I wore the crocheted beret again. I wondered if I should wear it one day and see what people said. I could plan a reunion lunch with my team from the ad agency, show up in the beret, and hand out nitrous-filled balloons. Maybe it wasn't as ridiculous as I thought.

Later on, back at our hotel room, I put the beret on and stared at myself in the bathroom mirror. The fluorescent light didn't help. *If I look like Joni Mitchell*, I thought, *it's like no version of her I've ever seen on any album cover or in any photograph.*

I left the hat in our hotel room when we checked out in the morning. I had already got what I wanted from it. And now it would just be another unwanted bit of nostalgia to carry to the End of the World.

CHAPTER 11

HOME ALONE

We took the long way, on a single-lane interstate instead of the more direct highway route to college, to the End of the World. We thought it would be more picturesque and allow us a calmer drive so we could talk. The three-hour trip went by in silence except for the random remark about a beautiful tree or a ray of sunshine that made the hills in the distance sparkle, or a noise that came from deep inside me that I couldn't stifle. I wondered how she felt about all the time we'd spent together. How did she feel about my neediness and about my desire to do everything with her? Was college the exit plan she'd been dreaming of for the past two years? The drive home was less quiet, however, on account of my relentless sobbing. A pile of wet tissues filled the passenger seat.

When I got home and opened the front door, I threw my bag on the floor and waited for my three dogs to notice I'd walked in. They eventually bounded around the corner to greet me. "She's at college," I told them. I wanted them to understand and pet me back. I wasn't hungry, but I thought I should eat. I wanted to be normal. It would be normal to eat dinner. I decided to make meatballs in tomato sauce. When my kids were all home, I always had a pot of meatballs simmering on the stove. It was an easy meal. I wanted meatballs. I wanted to eat to be happy. I wanted dinner to sustain me emotionally, not just fill my stomach. I wanted to feel full in every sense. I had nothing else to do. I had the time to make meatballs.

I thawed meat from the freezer in the microwave, grabbed a small handful of the slightly warm ground beef, added the requisite ingredients, and rolled a few balls. I threw them in a pot with oil and browned them. Next, I opened a jar of Rao's marinara and dumped it over the meatballs to let them finish cooking in the simmering sauce. The smell was soothing and tortuous at the same time. It brought back memories of family dinner at a time when I was alone and had no family dinners in sight. I thought about setting the table, with a place for my daughter, as if she were just running late. I knew my thoughts were on the edge of unhinged. *Stop it*, I told myself. *Get it together*.

When the meatballs were finished cooking, I ladled a few in a soup bowl to eat on the couch in front of the TV. During this process, I dropped one on the floor, and the white Maltese immediately stuck his face in it. I stared at the dog with his snout covered in marinara. I was unfazed. The larger spaniel pushed the little dog out of the way and gobbled up the meatball from the floor while the pug licked the sauce off the Maltese. I watched all this with complete disconnect. I was a fly on the wall in my own life. *If food drops on the floor, if there's a spill or mess in the kitchen*, I thought, *it doesn't matter. I'm just an observer. The dogs can figure it out. I don't have to worry. I don't even have to clean it up. I can be as messy and careless as I want. This is the bright side of being alone.* I thanked the pug for licking his brother clean.

Halfway through the trip to college, my daughter had turned to me several times in succession saying, "What?" I had no idea what she was asking me. She said I was mumbling. Saying things to myself. I told her I wasn't, and she said that I was driving and talking to myself so she interrupted because it was making her nervous, like I wasn't really there behind the wheel with her life in my hands.

"I don't know," I told her. "Just nervous, I guess." But I actually knew I talked to myself. I did it all the time. This was the just the first time I was caught doing it. Since the agency had closed, I was alone in the house most of the time. I was the only one I could count on to have a conversation with. I didn't realize I did it in the car, in front of her. She was the one person that I wanted to appear to be normal for—the one that I wanted to see me as reliable and stable and solid.

But I was caught talking to myself, and that made both of us worried. "I'll shut up," I told her.

"You can talk to me," she said.

"Right," I told her. Maybe I'd been mumbling about Levon Helm, or about eighteen-pound tumors, or maybe I was just running through my usual self-admonishments of regret and resentment for what my life had become. Whatever it had been, it hadn't been something to share with her. I concentrated with all my might to appear stable and strong. To be something like the mother she needed on a day that was supposed to be her day, but that I couldn't help seeing as mine. *Today is the beginning of my life alone*, I thought. Or who knows, maybe I mumbled it.

CHAPTER 12

PLEASE DON'T DIE

Laura Garza was killed in 2008. She left a nightclub in New York City with a guy she'd just met. After he suffocated her, he stuffed her body in a laundry basket before disposing of it in the woods. Court evidence said the murderer was a pervert. A sexual deviant. The prosecutors said he saw women as "an assembly of body parts and hair." There were forty-four examples of perverted or suspicious behavior presented in court. The month before he murdered Garza, he skipped three mandated sex-offender treatment meetings. Garza's mother kept her cell phone by her side for sixteen months after her daughter went missing. The day she got the news that her daughter's body was found, she turned it off.

I kept a mental note of murdered girls. I watched stories on the news of women who were killed—wives, girlfriends, mothers; women who were found in fields, woods, rivers, abandoned places—or never found at all. This is what it was like to be alone with my thoughts. This is how I filled my time, thinking I was being informed and aware. When I called my daughter at college for the first time to see how she was settling in, I told her about Laura Garza. Stories of abduction, rape, and murder became my primary form of communication with her. Our conversations were as dark as the abyss I was staring into. I tried to scare her into being safe at college. I used horrific stories as life lessons. She told me I made her feel like I thought she was irresponsible and reckless.

"Laura Garza thought she was safe with this guy," I said. "Look at Ted Bundy. He was said to be charming." Whenever my daughter told me about meeting someone or going somewhere with a new friend, I said something like:

"Don't get in a car with anyone you don't know."

"People are usually murdered by someone they know. You can't be too careful."

"There's safety in numbers."

"Don't walk alone after dark."

She very quickly decided that she didn't want to talk about her life at college with me. She didn't want to share her excitement and hopes, or the nervousness that she saw as exciting and new, not deadly. The topic of what was happening at school became all logistics. We talked about books, her professors, things she still needed for her dorm room, the forms that I repeatedly forgot to mail, and when she would be coming home for Christmas holiday.

When our calls ended, I pictured myself like Laura's mother, phone in hand and always on. Waiting.

CHAPTER 13

GONE BUT NOT FORGOTTEN

With my youngest daughter away at school, the sadness I felt at home escalated until she returned for Christmas break followed by a month-long winter internship. She was home until mid-February, which almost made me forget that she would once again be gone before I knew it. Instead of being thankful and enjoying her presence, I worried what would happen to me when she left again for campus.

Without her, no one was going to walk into the kitchen while I was cooking at the stove and ask me what smelled so good. No one was there to sneak up behind me and give me a hug or a kiss. Or wrap their arms around my waist and say, "I love you, Mom." When I thought I heard a noise and turned around to see who'd walked into the room, I knew no one was there. It would just be one of the dogs. Or nothing at all. The house settling. A creak. After she went back for her spring term, the front door didn't open anymore. There were no footsteps on the stairs. There was one plate and one fork and one glass in the kitchen sink that needed washing, night after night. I breathed in the silence and cried it out in tears.

Everything I did felt wrong. All my plants died. I had to constantly replace them. I shrunk clothes in the dryer. I burnt every piece of toast I made—the right toaster setting seemed to elude me. When I did see other people and attempt to join in conversations, no one seemed to hear me.

"I just said that," I told myself time and time again as I was passed over for my thoughts and remarks over someone else's.

I could sit home all day and not utter a single word aloud. Sometimes I would note to myself that I didn't speak once during an entire day. I was lonely and longed to feel someone's touch. I couldn't even remember the last time someone I met gave me a warm greeting and a hug. Until I saw X. He was someone I knew from my early days in New York City, post-college. I had bumped into him outside of a supermarket a few weeks earlier. It was a nice surprise to feel good about reconnecting with someone from a carefree time in my life. He was a hugger.

We went out for a drink. I listened for hours about his unhappy marriage, family issues, problems in general, and overall depression. We sat at a little round table and drank beer and did shots of whiskey. He was broke. I paid for another round. He was sad. I gave him a hug. He hugged back. It felt good. It was what I wanted. The place started to empty out. It was a weekday. Room at the bar opened up, and we relocated. Faster service. We had more beer followed by more shots. He pushed his stool closer to mine. He asked why we never got together when we were younger. He brushed a piece of hair from my face.

"Thank you," I said and smiled.

Here it comes, I thought. I didn't care that we were both drunk. I knew it wouldn't happen unless we *were* drunk. He was going back to his wife. I was going to remain alone. He leaned in. So did I. We made out at the bar.

"Let's go to your place," he said.

We spent three hours together. It only took three hours to make me feel loved, desired, smart, interesting, and exciting; three hours to feel like a teenager; three hours to have my brain and body come back to life. He said we should do it again. He said it didn't matter because he was going to get a divorce soon. I didn't care. This wasn't about him.

After he left, I constructed a fantasy of what it would be like to be in a relationship with him. He could move in with me. We could coordinate our schedules and say things like:

"See you later, at home."

"Want to meet up for a drink after work tonight?"

"Can you pick up eggs on your way?"

"Do you need anything washed?"

"Let's have brunch!"

I quickly wiped this from my mind, knowing that as my aloneness escalated, so did my panic for intimacy. This wasn't supposed to be about anything but touch and human contact and sex—sex that was supposed to relieve some stress and confirm that I could still be desired. It did the trick.

I was coasting downhill and didn't know where to turn for support. I was drinking more and more to numb myself. I would turn on every light in the house and put on *The Real Housewives*. I decided that reality TV star Lisa Vanderpump was my spirit animal. I wanted to be her and wipe my recent behavior out of my mind. I couldn't make images of me stumbling drunkenly around my room and waking up fully clothed on my bed disappear from my memory. So not Lisa. I wished I'd blacked out more so at least I wouldn't have to remember how out of control I was. I checked my email to see that the last eight messages I'd sent to my daughter in college had all gone unanswered. *She hates me*, I thought. *Or maybe she's just busy*, I reconsidered. *She is in college, after all, and has a lot of work to do*. I tried to console myself with this belief, but it didn't work. I decided to call her. She picked up unenthusiastically.

"Hey Mom, what's going on?"

"Nothing," I said, "I just called to say hi." She said hi back, which is all it took for me to burst into tears. "I'm sorry," I spat and began to sob uncontrollably. I told her I didn't know why I was crying and that I just felt so bad and missed her so much. I reminded her that I was all alone in the house with only the three dogs. I called them her brother and sisters to try and get her to laugh, but she didn't. I realized that there was nothing funny about this moment for me or for her. I continued to sob into the phone and blow my nose. She said comforting things like, "Please stop crying, Mama," and, "It will all be all right."

"I'm sorry I can't stop crying. I'm just so sorry."

She pleaded with me to stop crying. She said she had to go to class, so I needed to calm down so she could hang up. I tried to pull myself together for her. She told me to blow my nose. I listened. *She'll be a great mom one day*, I thought.

"I'm OK now." I told her I just needed to get it out. I said I knew that she thought I was having a midlife crisis. She said she loved me and that she'd call after class. I knew she wouldn't, but said OK and goodbye. I felt out of control, powerless, and lost. I felt like my daughter felt sorry for me and that this pity was, in itself, pitiable. I knew I had to pick myself back up...somehow.

I Googled "midlife crisis." 233 million search results were listed. *At least I'm not alone*, I thought. I began to like the idea of having a midlife crisis. It seemed like a normal thing. I needed to feel like there was a way out for me—that there was this tunnel called Midlife Crisis that I just needed to crawl through in order to come out on the other side, back to where I wanted to be, back to where I started. I liked the idea of being in crisis because that was at least something. Being in crisis meant that I had decisions to make and options to weigh. *A crisis is awesome*, I thought, *because at least conflict, confusion, and emotional turmoil over life decisions are better than the complete paralysis of hope and spirit that I'm experiencing.* A crisis, I concluded, was better than nothingness.

I thought about what variables I should consider in order to speed my way through the crisis tunnel. Should I buy the convertible or enroll in a six-week cooking school course in Florence, Italy? Tattoo or piercing? Shoes or bag? I started with deciding that I needed to call my daughter back so she could hear that I had truly calmed down. I wanted to tell her about my Google search and its ensuing epiphany, but I remembered she was in class. I felt alone again and imagined the next time she saw "Mom" appear on her phone screen that she would roll her eyes and say, "Ugh, I can't deal with this now." I concluded that she wouldn't come home during her next break and that she would stay at school for the summer too. I saw her drifting away into an abyss of avoidance and absence. I sat and stared ahead at nothing. Lips pursed. Eyes blank.

I was losing the ability to perceive myself as present. Even on the rare occasion that I saw other people, I avoided participating in conversations and dialogues. I no longer tried to connect. I just nodded and half-listened. I felt like an uninvited guest in my own body. I could barely remember who I had once been. I hated past-life reminiscences that began with the phrase "Remember when" because I could never remember when. I was always surprised to hear from my sister what my former self had done.

"Remember when we were kids and used to climb out the bedroom window onto the roof and hide? No one could find us."

"No."

"Remember when you wanted a leather jacket so badly that you put one on layaway for months? You worked every day after high school at Ben Franklin to get the money to buy it."

"No."

"Remember driving Grandpa's Cadillac convertible with the top down and the eight-track tape player blasting? You always wore a straw hat with a scarf attached that tied around your neck so it wouldn't blow off. You liked to sit in the back seat and sip Baileys Irish Cream from a small flask, while wearing white gloves."

"I wish."

None of this was even vaguely familiar. None of it sounded like me. This was the me that would have been sitting in front of my makeup mirror putting on blue eye shadow and pink blush, checking the light settings and magnifying imperfections that needed to be hidden. This was the me that wanted to dance. This was the me that was overdressed and overflowing with possibility and hope— out with my younger sister, trying to figure out the world, wanting to leave the small town we grew up in for something bigger. This was not the me that just threw away all of my bottles and tubes of makeup and skin care because they had expired over a year ago. They had never been used. This was not the me that made up reasons why I couldn't go out and needed to stay in for the weekend, every weekend. This was not the me who was always on the verge of a cold or flu and dressed in bulky layers for warmth and invisibility. This was not the me who wanted to crawl into my childhood bed and have my back rubbed so I could fall asleep.

One day my son called from Utah and after listening to me sadly whine, suggested that I do my version of *My Name Is Earl*, the TV show.

"Reconnect with your old friends."

"Make up with them for dropping out of their lives."

"Think about starting fresh," he said.

I figured that he didn't want me to visit again anytime soon. I flew to Utah to see him the summer after my daughter's first year at college—the summer when she rented an apartment in Vermont and didn't come home. We went to a rooftop bar in Park City with a bunch of his friends and drank Mind Erasers until we couldn't think straight anymore. I guess they worked. I continued by throwing back shots of whiskey for the amusement of him and all his friends. I acted like one of the undergrads instead of his mother. We ditched his car on Main Street and took a taxi back to his house. I imagined he wanted me to make a new friend and stop asking to come visit him.

"So you don't want me back?" I asked.

"It's not that. You're always complaining that you don't have anyone to do things with."

"I don't."

"So go make up with your friends; find some new ones."

"You think I'm a loser."

"I love you, Mom, and want you to be happy. Do what you want. You can always come here and hang out—not even a question."

This *My Name Is Earl* thing actually sounded like a good idea. Another TV show that I could model my life from. All *The Real Housewives* women did was fight with each other. At least Earl wanted to make up with people from his past and move forward positively.

Reaching out to people I basically blew off for years in the name of work and motherhood and general carelessness was hard. Or impossible. I made list after list of people I should reconnect with. I found most of them on Facebook, some on LinkedIn, and others I had email addresses for. I didn't want to call anyone. I was afraid of confrontation, of being bitched out and hung up on or, worst of all, just being ignored or blocked. I was scared. Email or messaging was the safer, more cautious (or cowardly) way to go. But I didn't do either. I looked at the list every day. I had the names on a sticky on my desktop. It became a constant reminder that I was more alone than ever. My past friendships seemed to be just that: past—something gone forever that I couldn't revive. *I should delete this sticky*, I thought every time I opened my laptop. But I didn't. It was self-punishment, and I believed I deserved it.

I caught my reflection in the mirror and saw something old and sad staring back at me. It was like a Hollywood makeup artist aged me for a role with a latex face mask complete with age spots, wrinkles, and an overall expression of lifelessness. My hair was pulled back in a ponytail with a few stringy strands greasily framing my face. *How is it possible*, I thought, *to have turned from someone who got up, dressed up, took the kids to school, went to work, and ran a business into this dirty, unkempt mess*? I thought about washing my face and hair, but even this proved too hard to initiate. Instead, I scooped up the dirty strands that were too short for the ponytail and tacked them up with a hair comb. *That's better*, I thought.

My days were starting to mimic each other and blur. Every day was like the day before. Every week was just like every other: I get up and go downstairs for coffee; I bring it back to bed and drink it while watching TV; I think about showering but don't; instead, I change my underwear and put on a clean pair of sweatpants and a T-shirt (I make sure my clothes are clean, since my body is not); I mindlessly watch TV in bed for a few hours; I feel hungry so I get in my car, drive to the deli, and order a turkey, lettuce, and mayo sandwich on white bread; I ask for the child size since it has less meat—I don't like that much meat on my sandwich; I bring it home and eat it in the kitchen in front of the TV, watching whatever; I do this for a few more hours.

Then, I try to accomplish things: I shop for food, or stuff much less necessary than food; I go to one of the three garden stores where I live and look at plants; I buy a new plant a week (I have a house full of plants, half of which are dying because I forget to water them); I putter around until dinnertime then open a bottle of wine and swill it as I make something to eat or order in; I keep the TV on in the kitchen and go upstairs to get back in bed—I like hearing the noise from downstairs because it makes me feel like I'm not alone; I turn the TV on upstairs too, finish my wine, and fall asleep.

CHAPTER 14

SMILE THERAPY

"Everyone thinks I'm sick," I told my daughter when we talked on one of the rare mornings she picked up my call. "I look like I have a permanent flu. Every time I go out and see people I know, they ask me if I'm OK. They look at me sadly and say, 'Oh, do you have a cold? So sorry.' I guess I look like I just rolled out of bed to get a container of soup and medicine from the pharmacy. Like I only emerged looking this shitty because I was in dire need of sustenance and medical supplies."

I seemed like an unwell person. My clothes were soft for comfort. My expression was lifeless. My mood was sullen. There were bags under my eyes, and my skin looked dull and dry. Fine lines had turned into full-fledged wrinkles. The kind that needs more than cream to make them go away.

My daughter had finished her first year at college and stayed in Vermont for the summer too, which I had predicted. I knew her winter break and internship at home were enough for her. I was not easy to be with. But she promised to come home for New Year's with her new boyfriend. Two months and counting and I would have her here again, and this time, I told myself, I would be the mother she expected.

"Maybe you should try to smile more," my daughter said kindly after seeing my inanimate expression on FaceTime. "There's something I read about called smile therapy. It's a real thing. All you need to do is smile, and it triggers hormones in your brain that help you feel happy."

"Why do I want to trick myself into feeling happy?" I asked her.

"It's better than nothing. It might be helpful."

"Helpful for what?"

"Just...life."

I went to the market to buy prepared food, and when I was checking out, I felt my eyebrows furrowing for no reason in particular. I immediately worried that my sadness might look like anger on my face. I burst into a huge smile to counteract my frown. The woman behind the counter looked at me quizzically and smiled back. It felt good. I felt happier in that moment. I thought there might be something to smiling. But by the time I got to my car and loaded in my bags of food, I could feel the frown coming back. One brief moment of uplift and already I was back on the floor.

I tried to find the words to explain how I felt each morning, waking up without a job to go to, without kids to mother and drive around, without people to talk to, without meetings and conference calls and lunch from the greasy take-out place across the street. I looked at the shower on my way downstairs, mentally noting that I would not be using it today or tomorrow or the day after that. I timed how long it took to make a Keurig coffee—pod to pour—and established four minutes as the approximate time I needed to be out of bed before crawling back in, hot coffee in hand. I propped myself up on three pillows, spread out my legs, then slumped to a half-sitting position. I watched myself do this maneuver in the blank, black screen of the large TV that popped up electronically from the foot of my bed when I hit the "on" button. I balanced my coffee on my stomach like it was a tray and stared at my reflection. I was too lazy to get an actual tray so my body would have to do. I continued to try and come up with words or phrases to describe how I felt. I wanted to say things like:

"This is the first day of the rest of your life."

"Now I can do all the things I've dreamed of doing."

"I'm making a bucket list and knocking it out."

Instead, I was only able to come up with single, meaningless words like:

"Fine."

"OK."

"Good."

I tried to find a clever, easy answer to "How are you?" which was becoming a very difficult question and one that rendered me speechless every time someone waited for a response. I thought about how I *really* was as I stared at my dark visage in the TV. Looking at myself this way, I knew that I was unlike any version of me that I had previously encountered. There was something dirty about my very being. Something a little grungy and spoiled, like rotting, clotted milk. It was a feeling that came from deep inside me, unaffected by any surface or physical change I made to my appearance. I imagined I smelled sour from every pore and fleshy fold. I could wash and perfume myself, but like Lady Macbeth, I could never feel clean. Was this lingering grossness the manifestation of who I was and how I treated people? Was it karmic revenge? I couldn't stop thinking about a conversation with an acquaintance I ran into at a business event, right before I stopped working.

"My, how the mighty have fallen," he said, when I let him know my business was going to close. He quickly tried to backpedal by saying he didn't mean it that way and that he just meant that he was sorry. He asked if he could get me a drink, and I said, "Sure."

"So you really think I have fallen?" I asked when he came back with my wine.

"I'm sorry. You know what I meant."

"No. Tell me."

"C'mon...don't make me feel bad."

"My, how the mighty have fallen," I repeated. "Well, at least the only place for me to go now is up," I lamely joked.

"Right," he said a bit too cheerfully.

I couldn't keep up the banter required for any further conversation. We couldn't get away from each other fast enough. I downed a few glasses of the free wine and left.

That had been about a year ago, but those words echoed in my head.

My, how the mighty have fallen.

I realized I couldn't shake this comment. It was stuck to me. It was a part of me—an extra appendage that was always there, in the way, in my line of sight, in my psyche. It was hanging from my side, slapping me with every step. Punishing me. *This is why I feel dirty*, I concluded. *I feel gross because I'm the cause of my own mess and undoing.*

My, how the mighty have fallen.

It was beginning to make a little sense. It was beginning to sink in. Memories from years and years of work life came flooding back, playing themselves out like videos on the blank TV screen that I was staring at.

I remembered a time when my assistant came into my office to update me on something that I had asked her to do, and I barked at her. I said, "I'm busy. I can't talk now. You should know better than to just walk into my office and interrupt me. Get out." And I remembered her face—it had the look of pain mixed with confusion mixed with sadness. That face has never left me. I couldn't shake how I made her feel. I couldn't shake the look on her face.

I remembered that I could have cared more.

I remembered that I had a temper.

I remembered that I pointed fingers.

I remembered scene after scene of my own shameful behavior, cringing and sinking further down in bed, under the covers and out of view of the TV screen. I pressed the power button on the TV remote to make it retreat down into its hiding place at the foot of the bed so I wouldn't have to look at myself anymore.

My, how the mighty have fallen.

One day, for no reason in particular, I tore through my closet and pulled out six fur coats. I called a friend who was selling vintage photographs and traded the fur for the photos. I felt smart for not spending any money and getting rid of dead animals for some nice prints. Success now had new parameters for me, I realized.

My, how the mighty have fallen.

I repeated to myself, "Tall and mighty, like the trees," over and over again, trying to willfully replace the phrase "How the mighty have fallen." I was still a tall, mighty tree that was not about to fall. This was something my daughter said to me, about me. She said I was strong like the big trees that surrounded our house. She told me to look out my bedroom window at those trees any time I needed to remember who I was. She told me the trees were strong and solid and that the reason they didn't break in a storm was because they worked with the wind to let it pass through their branches. I wanted to be like those trees. I wanted to feel strong. I wanted to show how impervious I was to being out of work and out of what I recognized as the normalcy of my life. I didn't want it to matter. I wanted to say, "Eh, no big deal. It's just part of life!"

Or I wanted to spout some truism like "The only constant in life is change" and cliché my feelings away.

But neither of these approaches was helpful or realistic. I felt more like a forgettable shrub than a towering pine. I tried to visualize myself as a one-hundred-year-old tree that had withstood seasons, storms, heavy snow on its branches, and droughts that caused dry leaves and peeling bark. I tried, again, to smile in the mirror and think of myself as a tall tree, all at the same time—two half-baked tactics for the price of one. I tried to reactivate my social life, to show off my tall and mighty self. Results were mixed. A woman I had dinner with one evening, an old friend, told me laughingly that she was wearing two pairs of Spanx—one to hold her in and one for extra confidence. I tried to laugh back. But it felt forced. I was immediately lost in my thoughts, reminding myself that people do all sorts of things to look and feel their best when out in the world. I asked her how she felt when she pulled them off at home.

"Relieved," she told me.

"You don't collapse on the bed in tears and sob until you fall asleep? You don't see your belly fat hanging in folds and begin to swear that you'll stick to a diet once and for all and never cheat?" I let out a manic laugh to signify that I was kidding. Kind of.

"Oh honey," she sighed.

I shook my head side to side and shrugged my shoulders with complete resignation to the fact that I couldn't even have conversations anymore without causing the people who loved me to feel concern and worry for my wellbeing. I couldn't even make a joke that didn't reek of self-pity and disgust.

I felt like I was starting to lose myself and my identity. I didn't even see my face anymore. My reflection distorted before my eyes, twisted into a jumble of worries and concerns. My entire being was composed of unflattering, unhappy adjectives. I was a giant word cloud of doubt and depression:

Fat

Old

Unworthy

Clothes don't fit

Why bother

Slouch too much

It doesn't matter.

I was beginning to disappear into my own head. I wanted to cover all my mirrors with black cloth and stop the clocks. I wanted to mourn the passing of the self I used to be. I promised myself that, in the future, when someone told me they were depressed or sad, I would never say the words "cheer up." I couldn't think of a more use-less and unhelpful suggestion. I was sick of hearing it. I felt ashamed for all of my own past lackluster efforts, the way I'd always deflected requests for help or advice from someone who was feeling down. I had been ignorant to the realities of depression and sorry for anyone that had ever come to me for assistance. I was unsympathetic and cold. I didn't get it. I wished I could go back in time, knowing what I do now, knowing how I feel now, knowing that I could never "cheer up" just because someone told me to. I had no reason or motivation to do anything except look in the mirror and gasp at what I had let myself become. Or, rather, what I would not let myself become. I didn't think I deserved happiness or joy or contentment. I could not "cheer up."

I thought again about my daughter's suggestion of smile therapy and, while looking in the mirror, lifted one corner of my mouth into a crooked grin. Then I lifted the other corner of my mouth into a creepy, tight-lipped Joker-ish version of a smile. I parted my lips and let my teeth show. It was an unnatural smile made up of three distinct facial moves, more muscle manipulation than happiness. I wanted to do better, so I started over and smiled at myself. I let a big, toothy grin burst across my face in one sudden, fluid movement. I turned my head from side to side and let out a fake laugh. It was the kind of laugh I imagined would emerge if someone said something complimentary that I could respond to with a giggle and grin: "Oh, thank you so much," I would say. "You're too kind." A few negative adjectives seemed to disappear from the mirror. The dark, unhappy word cloud lifted a bit. It wasn't much, but it reminded me of what being happy felt like. It reminded me that I needed to stop clipping my own wings if I was going to rise like a phoenix from the ashes of my doom and despair.

I thought about the woman at the store who had returned my desperate grin. I looked back at my image in the mirror, acknowledg-ing that my face and body reflected the pain I was feeling inside. I promised myself that I was finally going to try and smile today and see if it helped. I made a checklist of rules for smiling:

Make sure it's not fake-looking.

Make sure it's sincere. Don't smile randomly, for no reason.

Show teeth.

Laugh if appropriate.

Try not to look insane.

The next time I went shopping, I stopped by the Starbucks in the lobby of Target for a midday caffeine fix. I smiled at the person taking my order with true gratitude and thanks. It was definitely sincere. I needed that coffee. I smiled at people I passed in the aisles. Most smiled back. It was all very friendly, and it felt refreshing. I smiled throughout most interactions and encounters. I added a cheery "thank you" to the smile when it made sense. And it did feel good. It felt better than pushing my cart, head down, hoping not to be noticed or addressed. I passed the infants section and remembered my children as babies in their bouncy chairs, laughing and gurgling, kicking their pudgy legs as I played peek-a-boo with them. I remembered how easy it was to get them to laugh and smile. I thought about how thrilling it was to see little toothless grins appear back at me. *This is me now*, I thought. *I'm not a boss or a team leader or even a day-to-day mom anymore. I can't earn, command, or demand attention. No one is trying to make me happy.* I knew that I was the only one in charge of my own happiness. And like a baby, I was going to have to smile, coo, and wave my fists in the air if I was going to get anyone's positive attention.

CHAPTER 15

THE MEDIUM

It was a cold evening when I decided to take my newly practiced smile and attention-seeking baby antics to a crystal shop where a world-famous medium was going to help a group of us make contact with our deceased loved ones. As always, I hoped my grandfather would come through. We huddled in a semi-circle on folding chairs set up amid the shelves and display tables of the store. The medium was here as a stop on a promotional tour. *He looks normal*, I thought. *He doesn't look like some beaded-up shaman.* There were no flowing robes. No mala beads. His hair was short, and he looked like he could have just come from the office. He chatted as he got organized. He said that one doesn't choose to be a medium when one woman asked him how he got into all this. He said that being a medium was a calling, something he was compelled to do. He couldn't help it. Dead people just came to him.

Sure, I thought. *Why else would he be in this suburban crystal shop with fifteen women clutching at tissues and each other.* At 7:00 p.m. on a freezing cold night, a charlatan would have found something better to do, an easier way to make a buck. I felt confident.

The medium welcomed us and scanned the room. I gripped a tissue in my hand, ready to catch the tears I knew would come if my grandfather or Aunt Nell or anyone came through to me. I stared at the medium as hard as I could. I wanted him to feel my energy. I wanted him to bring me a message from beyond. He jumped right in.

"Is there anyone here whose name begins with the letter J? No?"

We all looked around at each other to see who would respond. Then, almost in unison, our heads snapped back to the medium waiting for his next communication.

"Is there a Pam or Patty or a P-name in the room? No...OK. Does anyone have someone who passed named Martin? There's a Martin here now. No? Well, Martin is here. Maybe he's just hanging around for a bit to see what's going on."

I continued to stare him down. *Feel my vibe*, I said silently to will his attention my way.

A gasp sounded from the back of the room. A woman said she was being choked. There was pressure on her neck. It was hard to breathe. The medium touched her shoulder and asked her what she thought was happening. She said her best friend had committed suicide by hanging. She thought her friend was reaching out. "She's here," the medium said. I wanted to raise my hand and ask him why a friend would connect this way. Why would the spirit want to cause her best friend this pain? Is this how spirits share? I wanted to ask him if spirits could cause you to gain thirty pounds and lose all self-esteem. I wanted to know if what I was experiencing was not my fault alone. "I'm here," I wanted to yell to the afterlife. "Connect with me. Choke me, if you must. Send me a sign that I'm worthy of reaching out to. Tell me if you've already reached out and I just missed it. Talk to me." The choking woman left the semi-circle to catch her breath. The medium connected with someone's father who said he was with her mother and was happy. Next, he connected with someone's son who passed on from a tragic accident. The woman whose son died cried uncontrollably. "I'm so sorry," said the medium. "Know that he wasn't in any pain when he passed." I sobbed, waiting for my turn.

He called out a few more names of spirits who were in the room. The store owner signaled to him that time was up.

The medium thanked us and said he would be in a nearby town tomorrow if we wanted to come and try to connect again. He told us there were books for sale at the register that he would sign. I put my soggy tissue in my pocket. It was wet with tears for others. No one came through to me. I glanced over at a woman on the opposite side of the semi-circle. I said hello to her on the way in. She had no idea who I was. I told her our kids had gone to school together. I told her my daughter's name. "Ah," she said. I realized that I was just as invisible to this world as I was to the next.

I was the last to leave. I was willing the medium to lift his head from the books he was signing, to look up, turn his eyes to me, and say, "Hey, there's a 'T' in the room now. It's your grandfather. He's sorry that he's so late, but he was taking your grandmother to church." I was afraid that if I left, I might miss a visit, a message. I stayed until the medium walked to his car. I followed him out the door. His car was parked in front of mine. I decided to talk to him as he was packing up.

"Hi...I was just inside with you," I said, trying out my new smile.

"Yes...how are you?"

"No one came through to me. Do you have any idea why? You didn't point at me or mention the name or initial of anyone in my life that's deceased."

"I'm not in control of who comes through," said the medium. "They just come."

"But why didn't anyone come through to me?" I whined.

"Maybe," he said, "they have nothing to say. Maybe there's no unfinished business with them on earth or with you. When spirits have nothing to say, they don't bother to connect. It takes a lot of energy for them."

"So no one connected with me because they have nothing to say to me?"

"Maybe." He closed his trunk and got in his car.

This confirmed that I was too dead for the dead to bother with.

I felt more alone than ever.

I looked at what the medium had inscribed in my book. It didn't make any sense.

"What does this mean?" I held the book up to the window of the car and showed him what he'd just written.

"I don't know," said the medium as he rolled up his window. "It's for you to interpret. I just write what comes to me."

He drove away.

I wanted to live my life like this.

"Hey, I just say what comes to me," I would tell people.

"You don't like what I said? Not my fault."

I, too, needed justification for the words coming out of my mouth. My older daughter, the one who'd had the eighteen-pound tumor removed before free-spiriting it out to the West Coast, told me I was becoming unsocialized, like an abandoned, neglected animal. She said I was spending too much time alone and forgetting how to act in public. She said I could barely follow a conversation and that my responses ranged from rude to irrelevant. *How great it would be,* I thought, *to respond based on the moment, like the medium did.* When you're being guided by the dead, everything is up for interpretation. I read once that another medium said she couldn't sleep because her bed was surrounded every night by spirits wanting to connect with loved ones. She saw them standing at the foot of her bed, just staring at her. She said it was unnerving. She had to yell at them and tell them to go away. She would sit up in bed and scream, "Leave! Get out." And they would go. I imagined them forlornly fading into the walls and curtains. Not everything that happened, I knew, was infused with hidden messages. I read the channeled inscription from the medium—"Let it shine. Let it shine. Let it shine." I wondered what the spirit world was trying to tell me.

CHAPTER 16

STEP OVER THE LOG

"When will you have arrived, in your mind?" my spiritually inclined friend asked me when we met for coffee. She was someone I turned to for advice. I liked her. I told her I would arrive when I stopped obsessing about every little thing that crossed my mind. I live in my head, I told her. I will have arrived, I thought, when I can once again follow a conversation and not have to say, "Can you repeat that?" because my attention had wandered away; when I can look at myself naked without harsh criticism; when I can think clearly and logically and stop excusing things I do, or don't do, by saying it was meant to be, or it's the universe talking; when I can remember what to hope for; when I can live in the present; when I can see a light at the end of the tunnel; when I don't have to begin almost every sentence with the words "You won't believe what happened;" when my daughter doesn't have to pick me up off the floor anymore.

She told me to imagine that I was walking down a beautiful path in the woods and that there was a log lying across the path, blocking the way. "Step over it," she said, "and keep walking. Every time a thought crosses your mind that you want to get rid of, imagine stepping over that log."

"That's it?"

"You can also kick the log off the path and out of your way, if there's something you want out of your life for good. And you can also sit on the log if you need to think a bit more about what to do."

"Step over the log," I repeated.

"It works. You have to visualize it very clearly. You have to see yourself, in your mind, stepping over the log."

"Do you ever kick or sit on the log?" I asked.

"I usually just step over it. It's enough. The repetition of seeing yourself do this will begin to become second nature, and it will help you quickly rid yourself of thoughts and feelings that you need to shake. It's also very useful when you run into annoying people—like the lady at the outdoor cafe who allows her dog to jump up on all the tables. I wanted to tell her she owed me a cup of coffee the other day, but I just stepped over the log and left in peace."

I can relate to this, I thought.

"Nothing," I said to my daughter when she asked what I'd been up to. I was pretty sure she wouldn't want to hear about my new stepping-over-the-log methodology. She thought I needed more help than talking to my smart and intuitive friend over coffee. She thought I needed to see a real professional.

"Nothing?"

"Yeah. Absolutely nothing. In fact, I'm not even busy doing nothing. I am literally doing nothing at all."

"Have you thought again about seeing a therapist? I think you really should consider it," she told me.

"I know. I haven't found one yet. I've been looking. That's actually what I've been doing."

"There are a lot in our area."

"I'll try harder," I said.

"You need to talk to someone."

Step over the log, I said to myself. My friend was right. It really worked.

CHAPTER 17

PSYCHIC-OLOGY

I agreed with my daughter that I should seek professional help for my anxiety and stress, but I wasn't through with the spirit world yet. I made an appointment for a tarot card reading. Gloria sat in a curtained corner of a spiritual bookstore in New York City. I booked her for a thirty-minute session. She said I could record it on my phone. I wasn't sure if I was going to like what she had to say so I declined. She asked me what I wanted to know about, and I told her nothing. I couldn't even think of one thing to tell her that I wanted to explore. "Let's just see what the cards say," I said. I really wanted to say, "You tell me. You're the psychic."

She told me that I was going to make a lot of money in the next few years. She told me that there was a man coming into my life, but he's not the "one" and not to fall for him. She wanted me to wait for another man who was coming a bit later. During the reading I learned that I needed to be careful in my decision-making; a creative period was coming, and I should trust myself. She asked if I had any final questions. I said no and thanked her for the reading. She thought I should come back again. She looked worried. I wiped away a tear and pushed past the curtains into the store. I bought a quartz crystal on the way out and put it in my pocket. She said I needed to connect with the earth more. She said I wasn't grounded. I wanted a second opinion.

Ann Marie was in her private room at the back of a store in the town where I lived. I had booked a thirty-minute tarot reading with her. She jiggled the bracelets adorning her wrist and, with a sweeping motion in the air over her bowed head, she snapped her fingers and asked for my angels and ancestors to let the cards show me the way. I cut the tarot deck in three with my non-dominant hand and put it back together.

"So what's going on?" she asked.

I told her about a dream: "A man named Giovanni and I are at a nondescript bar someplace having a beer with a group of friends. I don't know anyone named Giovanni. I'm wearing something strapless. I don't own anything strapless. I can't really remember what Giovanni looks like. He's dark-haired. He seems short. Giovanni's kissing me in a loving way and telling me I smell good. That's it."

She listened, nodded, and said, "Well, let's see what the cards say." She flipped four cards on her table, stopped, and looked at them. She asked me if I knew his sign.

I told her I didn't even know any Giovanni.

"His name might not be Giovanni," she said, "but you know him. There is definitely a man coming into your life." Four more cards flipped down on the table. "He's right here," she said, pointing to the Two of Cups, which is a relationship card. By the end of the reading, I had seven Major Arcana cards turn up. "You're going through a highly charged time in your life," Ann Marie told me. "And Giovanni is out there somewhere, so keep your heart and eyes open. You know him. Find out his sign and his birthdate when you figure out who he is. Then come back."

I felt elated at this news. The idea of having to look out for a man who I might know, who might be Giovanni, felt exciting. I wanted the reading, the cards, to give me answers. I wanted to believe that

I was destined for something. I wanted to be prepared for what might happen. I knew I could get stuck in a story that might never be written, but I wanted to try. So I called Y, someone I dated a few times, to see if he was my Giovanni.

We were sitting at a small table at the back of a neighborhood bar. It was a weeknight, after dinner, and we met for a drink. I could tell Y was trying to appear to be listening to my story. "The legend goes like this," I said over a glass of Sancerre. "My great-grandmother got very, very sick and went to the hospital. Back then, you only went to the hospital when you were going to die. It was 1969. So everyone knew when the doctor said she had to go to the hospital, things were bad. She was there for about a week and then she died. My great-grandfather came home from her funeral, got into bed, and never got up again. He died a year later, almost to the day of his wife's death. And then, when their son—my grandfather—came home from his father's funeral, he cleaned up dishes, threw out all the food that would go bad, and locked up the house for good. It's like he wanted them to be able to go back to their home in death, like it was in life. Their clothes were still in their closets. My great-grandmother's hair brush was still on the dresser where she left it the day she went to the hospital, her hair still in it. And my great-grandfather's hat was still on the hook where he hung it when he came home from his wife's funeral. Isn't this the most beautiful love story you have ever heard? When it's your time to die, don't you want someone that loves you so much that they give up their body to travel through space and time to be with you?"

Y nodded and ordered two margaritas. "The best I can do is make love to you all night."

"I'm good for about thirty minutes," I replied.

"Drink up," he said.

When I slithered into bed at his place, I got on all fours and buried my head in the pillow. I couldn't look him in the face.

"Wow," he said while unzipping. "Most girls hate this position."

When I rolled back over, it was 1:30 a.m. He was already snoring. There were six texts and three missed calls from my daughter.

"Shit," I whispered. "The one night she decides to call me, and I'm somewhere on all fours." I threw on my clothes and left.

My phone rang early the next morning.

"Mom. Are you okay?"

"Yes."

"I've been worried."

"Sorry. I had a dinner that went late." I tried to act like nothing was wrong.

"I was really scared."

"I'm sorry. I should have texted you, but I just got caught up."

I wanted to tell her that I got caught up in trying to feel alive and loved. That I got caught up in wanting to be touched and hugged and kissed. That I didn't return her calls because I was dreaming of a life that wasn't fueled with margaritas and wine and lying to her and rolling over on my stomach to have sex because it was as meaningless to me as it was desired. But what I actually said was that we could talk later because I still wasn't fully awake.

I messaged Y and asked him for his astrological sign.

CHAPTER 18

CRYING AT THE GYM

Unsuccessful attempts at doing things that I should have succeeded at made me feel broken. I couldn't even get the simplest things right. My daughter asked me what I got my mother for Christmas. "A box of really nice chocolates," I told her.

"Grandma has diabetes," she reminded me. I ate the chocolates for dinner over the next several days, almost as punishment for how careless and thoughtless I was. The word "Mom" was crossed off my Christmas list. I added her back on.

No one knew what was happening to me because I disguised my depression under baggy clothes, excuses, and my new fake smile. No one knew how I felt or what I was doing when I was alone. No one knew that what I said I was doing was not the truth. I realized that when I told a few people what I had actually been up to—the medium, the psychics, having visions of my dead grandfather—they winced, then whimpered in sadness for what I had become. So I hid my turmoil, regrets, and depression from everyone. I put on a stiff upper lip when I needed to emerge into the world to shop for food or things I needed around the house, then retreated back home, under the covers. I didn't want to feel this way. I didn't want to live one life in the world and the opposite at home. I felt torn by who I was and who I wanted to be. I wondered how the imposter Christian Gerhartsreiter, alias Clark Rockefeller, had successfully managed his competing personas. I wondered how he reconciled being a rich Rockefeller by day with his former-German-exchange-student and wanna-be-actor reality. He used murderer David Berkowitz's social security number to get a job. He lived the life of a wealthy scion. He married a successful, intelligent woman. He faked who he was and fooled a lot of smart people. I faked it every day too.

I dreamed time and time again about being someone I wasn't.

I wanted to be the person that people talked about as having it all.

"Some people have all the luck," they would gush!

I wanted to be the one who thinks everything is going to work out, and it does. I wanted to feel like the construction worker on a broken scaffold who cheated death, or the kid that fell seven stories and lived. I wanted to be the woman who escaped her attacker, or the drug addict that was found in time and lived to shoot up another day. I wanted to be gung ho with positivity and optimism, able to make things happen out of sheer willpower, energy, and stamina. I wanted to feel triumphant. Instead, I sat on the floor of Equinox gym and tried to hold together the façade that was me. My trainer asked me to get into a plank position and hold it for fifteen seconds. I held it for three and collapsed. Then I burst into tears.

"I can't," I wept.

"It's OK," he said as he joined me on the floor. Another trainer came over, thinking I was hurt. My trainer waved him away.

"I'm so sorry. This is so embarrassing."

"Don't worry," he said, trying to lighten things up. "This is nothing. You should see the stuff that happens here."

I wiped my nose with my sleeve, and he pulled me up.

"How was your day?" my daughter asked when we next spoke.

"I sat on the gym floor and cried because I couldn't do a plank. I act like a workout buff to everyone, talk about going to the gym, getting fit, eating healthy, but none of it's true."

"Really?"

"Really," I confessed. "That is the best summation of how I'm doing. And I cried loudly too. It was not a whimper. It was full-on wailing. People were looking at me like I was hurt or crazy. Trainers came over to help. I looked up at one sobbing and told him I couldn't do a plank. He backed away like he was retreating from a rabid animal."

"Sorry, Mama."

"Do you know how many times you say 'Sorry, Mama' to me? Too many. I'm sorry. I'm the sorry one. I am so sorry that I make you say that to me. I'm sorry that that's all you can say to me." My tone was frantic. I was ending my sentences in a high-shrieked pitch. I sounded angry. And I was. But not at her.

I wondered if this was how alias Clark Rockefeller felt when he got found out.

I made an appointment with a psychic named Wanda who specialized in messages from angels. When I sat across from her, she told me that I had angels surrounding me. She said that they were there to help me. She said I was going through a highly charged time. *I've heard this before*, I thought. Wanda said that I needed to ask the angels for help. She said they needed my permission to intervene.

"Should I pray to them?" I asked her.

"Just ask them to help you," she said. "Tell them what you need and want."

"So it *is* like praying," I pressed on.

"If asking is like praying to you, then yes."

Was asking like praying for me? I knew I was often praying for things that weren't likely to happen. I decided that my angels weren't intervening because my requests must have been just as unanswerable as my prayers.

I prayed that the pile of clothes on the floor would get up and put themselves in the laundry basket. Or better yet, in the washing machine.

It did not.

I prayed that time would move in reverse because there was so much I missed the first time that I could now make right.

It did not.

I prayed that I could get up and function like a person who has much to be thankful for.

I did not.

I prayed to be saved but didn't specify what from. I wondered if my angels could at least figure out that much without my asking.

They did not.

CHAPTER 19

CAT'S OUT OF THE BAG

I met someone for lunch at an Italian restaurant with an outdoor seating area. It was a nice spring day. I didn't know her very well and can't remember how we met. I decided to accept her invite to get together. *Why not*, I thought. *My son did tell me to make friends.* Next to our table were two men trying to sell the restaurant owner a new brand of vodka to serve at the bar. I was on my third glass of rosé. The owner was walking back and forth between talking with the men, making sure food was coming out the right way, and seating people in the restaurant. One of the salesmen leaned over our table and asked if we wanted to try the vodka. He signaled the waiter for two shot glasses.

"Tell the owner if you like it. It's the best vodka on the market today," he said.

We each did a shot. It tasted like any other vodka to me.

We did two more shots each and ordered two more glasses of rosé.

The owner brought us his special limoncello at the end of our long lunch, which lasted until about 4:00.

I don't remember getting home.

I do remember that when I woke up about 10:00 to use the bathroom, I saw my purse on the bathroom floor. I thought it was weird that it was there and not in my closet. I picked it up. It was filled with my puke.

The next morning, my mother posted a comic on her Facebook page. It was a photo of a cat at a bar drinking. The caption read, "Who is this Moderation person everyone says I should drink with?" She tagged me. I decided it wasn't just a coincidence, that she must know how much I was drinking. She'd been asking too many questions about what I had been up to, how I had been spending my days. She made too many comments about how late I was sleeping in.

I liked her post.

CHAPTER 20

YOU MUST CHANGE YOUR LIFE

I lacked concentration. I couldn't focus. My mind wandered between reality and fantasy scenarios. One moment I daydreamed that I was giving a TED Talk in front of an applauding audience and felt hopeful. The next minute I blinked it away to see an image of myself in bed watching TV and felt sad. I needed to get a hold of my thoughts and fears. I wanted to be productive and feel mindlessly busy to help quiet the emotional roller coaster I was on. I decided to clean out rooms and closets and get rid of things that were no longer used or needed. I could deal with a garbage bag of clothes in the corner of my closet that needed to go to Goodwill. I could open my mail and throw away the old newspapers that sat in a pile on a kitchen credenza. I could tear through my children's abandoned rooms and get rid of things I thought they no longer needed. I emptied drawer after drawer, shelf after shelf.

I decided to have a yard sale and get rid of the pieces of furniture that held sadness and regret in their fabric. I couldn't look at the couch where my daughter had once sat crying over something. Or the chair my son always used to sit in to watch TV. The bed I'd snuggled in night after night with my kids when one of them was sick or couldn't sleep had to go. I replaced these things with new pieces devoid of wear and memory. I wiped the slate clean. It helped a bit. Instead of saying, "That's the chair my son always used to sit in," I said, "That's where the chair that my son always sat in used to be." It was an arm's length removed from my grief.

I found a photo of my older daughter from high school graduation. She's standing under a tree with her friends. They're all wearing white wedding gowns. I wished I remembered that day in more detail. I don't know why I didn't. I felt like my memory was slipping away. I thought about a day not very long ago, when I'd gotten in the car to drive to the store and somewhere along the way completely blanked out as to where I was going. I didn't know what lane to get in or where I needed to turn. I kept driving straight ahead until, all of a sudden, I remembered that I was supposed to be picking up dinner.

I pulled a small book of poetry by Rainer Maria Rilke from a shelf that I was in the process of reorganizing. I'd bought it for one of my graduate school classes. There was a poem I loved: "Archaic Torso of Apollo." I opened to it and read it again. I had read it many times before. *It's now about me*, I thought. *Or it could be about me.* I felt like the old statue Rilke was describing. I was headless, blind, and broken. I felt like something had happened to me and that I didn't even know what that something was. I didn't know what had caused me to end up in this damaged condition.

The last line of the poem seemed to come out of nowhere.

You must change your life.

This has to be a sign, I thought. *Would it be bad luck to ignore it*? So far, none of the things I'd thought were signs had gotten me anywhere, but maybe this was different? There was no one to run this thought by. I couldn't ask my daughter who already saw me as untethered. I knew she was tired of lifting me up when I collapsed in tears for no reason or many reasons. I couldn't tell her that I thought this poem was an omen of some sort. I couldn't tell her that it was the first thing that had given me hope in a long time. I wanted to tell her that a billowing curtain is not always because of the wind and that I needed to pay attention to what crossed my path. I realized that I had been walking through my waking hours not really seeing or hearing anything. I heard this message loud and clear. *There is nothing worse than a missed sign or signal*, I concluded.

You must change your life.

Yes, I thought. *I must change my life.*

The tattoo parlor was up a long flight of stairs on West Fourteenth Street in New York City.

I told the woman at the desk I wanted a line of text down my arm and asked if there was anyone available. "Yes," she said, and told me to write the line down on a piece of paper.

You Must Change Your Life.

I handed it to her with a big smile.

"This is what I want."

"OK. Do you know what type of lettering?"

"It's from a poem," I said.

She handed me two binders.

"You can choose from anything in these books. Here are some forms, and it's cash only."

I asked her if I could discuss the font with the tattoo artist. I wanted confirmation, not procedural efficiency. I wanted joy and delight in my decision to have these words etched into my skin. I told the tattoo artist I wanted it to look like something I just scribbled, frantically, in haste—like an idea that just came to me and that I had to write down before I forgot it. He suggested we do it in red to indicate urgency and passion. "Yes," I said. "I love that idea."

You Must Change Your Life.

It took about ten minutes. "You Must Change Your Life" stretched between my wrist and elbow on my left arm. He told me how to care for it, and I walked down the long stairs and into the street feeling like a new person, like the kind of person who could really change.

"Guess what," I said to my daughter.

"What?"

"I got a tattoo yesterday."

"Oh no. Show me."

I pulled up my sleeve and exposed my forearm to her on FaceTime.

"That's Sharpie!"

"No. It's a real tattoo."

"I don't believe you."

I told her I couldn't ignore this thing that happened when I was cleaning out the house. I told her I was going to be inspired by these words every day. I told her I loved it.

"So, what now?" she asked, like she was therapizing me.

I didn't know. I immediately regretted showing the tattoo to her. *I should have hidden it for a while,* I thought. *Now she thinks I'm losing it. Seeking in vain. Trying uselessly.*

I began to worry that my actions were giving away how sorry I was feeling for myself: *Boo-hoo, you-need-to-figure-things-out-type sorry; Boo-hoo, your-kids-are-growing-up-like-all-kids-do-type sorry; Boo-hoo, there's-no-one-you-can-talk-to-at-home-anymore-type sorry.* I felt leaden. Moving my body was an effort. My arms each weighed one hundred pounds; the tattoo had done nothing to change that. I could barely raise them over my head to get a glass from the kitchen cabinet. I had frequent visions of myself lying on the floor, unable to move, with no one around to find me. To save me. Perhaps this should have been a happy time for me. I was free of the day-to-day tasks of raising children. I was free of the anxieties of a job. I was free of everything that had once demanded my time. If I didn't want to cook, or eat, I didn't have to. I could shop for what I wanted without worrying about who would or wouldn't like it. I could be my only focus, and it could be great. I could start that book I kept promising myself I would write. But the tattoo lay dormant on my arm. The command went unheeded. I carved it into my skin hoping it would create a new me, but it didn't. Maybe nothing could?

CHAPTER 21

I'M GOING HOME

I was lost and the only way to get unlost, I thought, was to go home to the place where I grew up. I wanted to take the crystals out of my pants pockets and admire them for their beauty, not carry around rocks for energy and inspiration. The tarot reader at the bookstore told me I needed them, but they were weighing me down. All my superficial attempts to change my life were bricks, not wings. I needed to heal. I needed to sober up and stop drinking myself into oblivion. I needed to be a better mother and better person.

I drove past the four-story, green-shingled house on the corner lot that once belonged to my maternal great-grandparents, whom everyone called Mom and Pop. Nine of us lived there, sleeping on couches, beds tucked into attic corners, or in one of the three actual bedrooms. I lived within a loving extended family consisting of my great-grandparents, my grandparents, my great-aunt and uncle, my mother, and my younger sister. It was the mid-1960s in upstate New York. We all had our meals in the shared kitchen in the basement, which opened onto a small arbor of concord grapes with a flower garden a few steps beyond. We had a big all-family pancake breakfast every Sunday after church. Even the slightest whiff of buttermilk pancakes or sausage cooking in a cast-iron skillet brings me back to this time without fail. My sister and I were doted on. My great-aunt Nell and great-grandmother Blanche played board and card games with us by the hour, helped us make cookies and brownies, cleaned up all the messes, and then patiently followed us around the house and yard as we moved onto our next activity. There was no actual father in my life, but I had seven parents, which was more than anyone else I knew had, and that was OK with me. And the extended family didn't end there. A few blocks away lived my grandmother's sister, Aunt Beanie, with her husband, two sons, and my other great-grandmother, who had gone blind from glaucoma. On weekends and summers, I could have breakfast at one house then head over to the other for lunch. In between, almost anything could happen.

I wanted to feel like that child again. That child who was unconditionally loved and admired—that child who wandered freely and was welcomed everywhere with hugs and kisses.

"I'm just a girl. I'm just a girl that grew up," I said to my daughter. "I'm having a hard time, and nothing is getting better. I may seem brave on paper, but in reality, I can't face people anymore. I can't look people in the eye. I say things like 'oh stupid me' and put myself down when I don't feel like I measure up, which is all the time. I avoid conflict with you, your brother, and sister, which means that I'm not being the mother I should be. We aren't friends. I'm your parent. I forget this a lot. I'm constantly walking on eggshells with all of you. I never push back. Challenge. Ask a question. Do you know that I'm scared all the time? I sleep with clothes and shoes in a pile on the floor next to my bed so in the middle of the night, I can get dressed and run out of the house at a moment's notice. I'm constantly ready to run away. To escape, evacuate. I can't be who you need me to be because I'm so scared. The people I loved growing up have all left me. I was raised by three generations, and now they're gone. There's just my mother, and she's getting old now. I'm always scared that you'll never come back. And if that happens, I'll pick up my clothes from the floor, get dressed, and walk out the door. I don't want to live like this anymore. I don't want to be sad. I want to be a happy baby."

When I walked into my old bedroom in my mother's house, I cried uncontrollably. It all came at once, when I least expected it. I was engulfed in sadness so intense that it felt like relief. The rush of calm I had from sitting in my childhood room, looking at my scattered mementos and memories, faded fast. I eyed my desk lamp and the blotter I used throughout my school years, scribbled on as if I just took a note or captured a thought. There was a wooden keepsake box that every high school senior got for free from a local store, placed just where I left it. Inside the box were old photos, a pin, my college dining hall cards, and an old school ID. There was a newspaper clipping of me out at an event with friends, and an article I'd written for a local publication. I curled my toes in the orange-and-green carpet that I remembered picking out when I was ten years old and lovingly breathed it all in.

My frame immediately stiffened. I had allowed myself to feel happy for a moment, and now this was the result. I felt a deep pain in my right shoulder. My body was revolting. Tears came rolling out, reminding me that I was not allowed to feel joy, or respite, or anything but complete and utter dismay. I realized that I saw everything as a problem. Problems were all I had left. My dramas, messy stories, fits, inner turmoils, and hysterical crying were what defined me. Crying felt normal. It made me feel like me. I wasn't even worthy of reminiscing about being happy, let alone seeking it in the present.

I sat in front of my make-up mirror to wipe my eyes. It was on the dresser, in the same place my thirteen-year-old self used to sit. I was transported back in time. I saw four big-eyed cat prints framed on the walls over my desk. I saw a globe that I used to spin when I was bored and doing homework. I saw a burlap wall hanging with the words "God Is Love" cut out in blue felt and glued on. I'd made it in Sunday school. I saw my great-aunt Nell sitting up in bed behind me.

I cried harder. I cried with regret and remorse and longing. This room wasn't mine and hadn't been mine for a while.

After I moved out, it was given to my grandfather's aunt, who needed full-time care. It was my Aunt Nell's room with some of my stuff still hanging around. I remembered seeing her in my old bed when I would come home to visit. Sometimes she knew who I was; other times, she was just happy to have company. I remembered that she always recognized a sparkly marcasite hair clip that she gave me. I put it in my hair whenever I sat with her. She knew it was her clip. She reached her hand up and touched it when I brought my head close to the bed and showed her. "See," I would say, "I'm wearing the hair clip you gave me. I love it." I can still feel her soft hand with its skin so thin and fragile rub my cheek and tell me how beautiful it looked in my hair. I wished I still had it.

I continued to stare in the mirror, past my puffy, red eyes and tear-stained cheeks. I saw my teenage self, sitting here putting on make-up as I was getting ready to go to a party or school event. I remembered that when I was allowed to wear make-up to school for the first time, I asked for a lighted make-up mirror for Christmas. It was all I wanted. The mirror had a slide at the bottom that allowed me to adjust the light based on the environment I was getting made up for—day, night, home, or office. It was two-sided for regular and magnified viewing. It made me feel grown up. It made me feel in control. Now I wished I had a new make-up mirror—one that would show me false hopes, misplaced affirmations, and missed signals. I wanted to pick up the phone and call one of my friends to commiserate. But there was no one I could call. There were no childhood friends because I didn't keep in touch with anyone from home. I had moved away and left everyone behind. Including myself.

I flipped the mirror to the magnification side and looked at my eyebrows. I remembered when I plucked them for the first time. They never grew back right. I saw a mark from the second hole in my ear-lobe that I pierced myself, in this mirror, when my mother told me

I couldn't get another piercing. I numbed my ear with a piece of ice then stuck a sewing needle through it. I walked downstairs and said, defiantly, "See, I just did it myself." I remembered putting on blue eye shadow, blush, mascara, and lipstick—more make-up than I'd worn in years. I remembered flipping open the pages of *Seventeen* magazine to try out the latest beauty tip. I made a facial mask using a beaten egg and honey and sat here, slathering it on my skin. I watched it harden and tighten around my mouth until I couldn't move my lips to talk anymore before walking to the bathroom to rinse it off.

I turned the mirror off and pushed it back on the dresser. I couldn't face myself. I was no longer thirteen. And I was no longer Coco Chatterly, the nom de plume I was given by a mischievous editor to write a monthly New York City social calendar, one of my first jobs after college. I knew why Coco suddenly came into my thoughts—she would have loved this mirror. She was out every night, going to clubs and parties. She was putting on make-up, dressing up, and meeting friends. Now I was thirty pounds overweight, with ill-fitting clothes and a face so bloated that there weren't enough settings on my mirror to lend any light to my situation.

I began to realize that I hadn't been happy for a long time. Longer than I had thought. I tried to recall a moment of unabridged joy over the past two years and couldn't muster up a single one. I couldn't face myself in the mirror anymore. I knew when I was indulging in mocha ice-blended coffee with extra whip that I would pay for it somehow, but it had all happened so fast. Thirty pounds and counting. One day my pants fit, and the next I couldn't get them buttoned. My jeans wouldn't close. I walked around for a while with the top button undone, hidden under a baggy sweater. But even that little maneuver had become impossible as I continued to gain weight. I'd taken to rooting around in my son's closet, digging out old pairs of sweatpants from his high school days. They reminded me of him and they fit. This felt like success.

As I stood in my childhood room, I realized that I was heavy in both body and mind. I wore regret and sadness like a jacket weighted with chains. I was Jacob Marley, dragged down by what my life had become. I was shackled, tormented, and doomed. My shoulders slouched. My posture was horrible. Everything about me submitted to gravity. I tried to stand up straight, but it was too much of an effort. I adopted the posture of putting one arm behind my back like a stance of a well-mannered, old-school gentleman—someone from another world, another generation—trying to force my shoulders back to an upright position. I sucked in my stomach and pushed out my butt. I looked at my profile in the mirror as I went through a series of posture corrections that all resulted in the same slouchy, Neanderthal stoop. I remembered a recent routine doctor's visit. The nurse had looked me up and down and said, "You're about five foot seven, right?"

"No," I said, "I'm six feet tall." I realized that I was being weighed down. I was diminished by five inches. I was literally failing to measure up to myself.

I looked around my old room. I wished my Aunt Nell was there touching my hair and smiling up at me. I wished my grandfather would walk in and tell me it was time to get ready for school. I wanted to hear my grandmother yell goodbye up the stairs as she ran out the door for church, always in a hurry. Always just a little late. I longed for the people in my life that were gone from this world. I missed them. I wanted them back. I closed the keepsake box and unplugged the make-up mirror.

I wanted to move forward with my dreams, but my dreams consisted of going back in time—to my childhood, to my kids' childhoods, to a past I could not relive. I don't know how I had never fully considered what my life would look like when my children grew up and left. I don't know why I had never pondered what being alone would feel like and what I would be doing. I hadn't planned for this part of my life. I hadn't even thought about it. Instead, I fantasized about myself as an enchanted being. I envisioned myself as someone who was always happy and carefree, walking from place to place, room to room, smiling, humming, getting organized, completing tasks, and waiting for my little ones to come home for dinner. In this fantasy, I was always whistling and looked a little like Snow White. But what finally began to sink in was that I was all alone, with nothing but my children's three empty rooms, and three hungry dogs, in a cold, dark house. The only thing that could help me forget, escape, avoid was my special glass emblazoned with the words "Mama Needs Some Wine," filled to the very top.

I stuck my knitting needles into the ball of yarn I was using and put it away, high on a closet shelf. "I can't do this anymore," I sighed. I had taught myself to knit from a YouTube video. I only knit scarves because they were the most mindless of options. I could knit a scarf while watching TV. This made me feel productive. I kept a basket full of yarn and knitting needles next to my bed. I knit scarf after scarf. Some were better than others. I had a drawer full of subpar scarves that no one really wanted, including me. The problem was that I lost interest halfway through each one and none of them were long enough.

"The scarf is a little too short for me," my daughter laughed after she unwrapped a green-and-white version I had just mailed to her. "It doesn't wrap around my neck."

"Right," I said. "I can make it longer. Send it back."

"No, that's OK, Mom. I Just wanted you to know that you need to make them a little longer generally."

CHAPTER 22

JESUS WILL SAVE YOU

I tried to ask myself, "Remember when you had a life worth living?" But I couldn't bring myself to answer this question. I decided I needed to get away and force some feelings out into the open. I didn't want to be in familiar surroundings where I could easily distract myself with busywork. I planned a weekend of nothing in upstate New York. I wanted to hibernate in a hotel room, lick my wounds for my closed business and childless existence at home. I wanted to rest exposed on the bed and face everything I was feeling. I wanted to commit to the words, thoughts, and emotions that I couldn't say aloud to myself or others. I wanted to confess exactly how I got to this point. Deep down inside, I was sure I knew. I thought I could sit in a hotel room and force it out. On the surface, I couldn't—or wouldn't—articulate it. I needed to speak the truth, and I wanted to do it alone in an anonymous place where I could cry without anyone noticing or caring, without anyone looking at me with worry and concern. I would shield my raw, red eyes from strangers, hiding behind dark glasses whenever I emerged into the light for food and coffee.

I had settled into my room and was walking on the street to get some air and a bite to eat when I saw two young women coming toward me on the sidewalk. As we approached each other, one of the women said she liked my coat. We exchanged smiles. "Thanks," I said.

"Do you have time for a quick question?" one of them asked me.

"Sure."

"Great. Ok. So, what makes you happy in life?"

"Nothing."

The two women exchanged glances then stared back at me in silence.

"Service to others," one of the women said, "will give your life meaning."

"Doubt it," I said flatly.

"Would you like to talk about it?" they asked.

"No. I'm going through a hard time, and I need to be alone. I need to work things out for myself. I've always been self-sufficient, and I need to get back to that. I cry every day. It's not healthy. They aren't tears of joy. My youngest child moved out for college, leaving me all alone. My business folded, and I'm out of a job. I have to face myself, by myself, for the first time in years. I have no friends because I blew them off in the name of work and kids. I have no one to talk to or turn to. I'm here in this town to seek solace. I'm on my way to get some food then go back to my hotel room to scream into a pillow."

"Jesus will save you," one of the women said.

The other handed me a postcard and told me they were sister missionaries from the Church of Jesus Christ of Latter-Day Saints.

I told them to have a good day, and we continued on our ways.

I called my daughter to tell her I scared away two missionaries.

"That's quite a feat," she said hesitantly.

"What did you say to them?"

"I just told them you left home to go live your life, and I was a little sad."

"That doesn't sound very scary."

"I may have also said a few other things. But what I really want to tell you is that I think I'm going to church on Sunday when I get

104

home. I think they may have a point. Maybe Jesus will save me. Someone has to, for fuck's sake."

I used to say my prayers every night before I went to sleep. My grandfather and grandmother stood next to my bed after tucking me in and listened to me recite, "Now I lay me down to sleep, I pray the Lord my soul to keep," then list all the names of my relatives, friends, and pets that I wanted God to bless. I said my prayers that night in the hotel room for the first time in years and cried myself to sleep. I used to be afraid not to say my prayers. I was worried that not praying would cause something bad to happen. I don't know when I stopped praying. I thought it might be why I was in this position. I wanted to pray again. I thanked the sister missionaries in my prayers that night for reminding me of this.

I came back home from my trip upstate feeling freshly inspired and uncharacteristically unburdened. I responded to Z who had, by chance, texted me to see if I wanted to meet for a drink and said, "YES." Z was at the bar sipping a glass of red wine when I arrived. He ordered me one.

"No thanks," I said and asked for tequila on the rocks. He called me hardcore and said he liked it. I thought I saw him lick his lips. We sat down at a table and ordered. We made small talk. He had never been to this restaurant before. He was definitely coming back. Did I want wine with dinner or was I going to stick with tequila? He was having a party next week that I should come to. He's usually vegetarian, but the salmon looked too good to pass up. His kids were amazing, and his ex-wife was a cunt. She was crazy. He was in love with her once but not anymore. He dated a lot and hey, why not, he was a single man. Finally, he asked me what I'd been up to lately.

"I went to church for the first time in a long time," I told him.

"Why?" He was shocked. He scowled at me.

I started to tell him the story of the sister missionaries and how that encounter made me think that I needed prayer, and God, and this kind of hope and belief in my life again. He cut me off.

"You don't *really* believe in God, do you? I mean you don't believe there's a guy up there in the sky looking down? Right?"

"I'm not sure what you mean," I said. I could have told him about how I had stopped the sister missionaries in their tracks, how they had never encountered someone like me before. I could have joked that I was surprised they didn't call 911 and have me committed to the psych ward. But I didn't. I wanted to end this dinner.

He told me that he was surprised that someone like me would believe in God.

"Someone like me," I repeated.

"Yeah," he said. "Someone smart."

I asked him, if his son were in a car accident and it was a life-and-death situation, would he pray?

"Not to God," he said.

"Who would you pray to, then?"

"Not God. Anyone but God. I don't know—the earth, the sky. But more importantly, I would get the best doctors money could buy and pray to myself to figure this out. I would save my son. I wouldn't leave it up to a God that doesn't exist."

I told him that I would pray and pray and pray to God. I told him that if one of my children were on the verge of death, that I couldn't *not* pray, that I would not be able to avoid prayer, and, in fact, it would probably take over my existence as I sat next to the hospital bed, holding hands and wishing for a voice to emerge from the silence and say, "Hi, Mom."

"Then your kid would probably die," he said.

"No," I said. "No, no, no. None of my children would ever die from prayer, or hope, or wishing, or putting goodness into the world. Yes, I would make sure they got the best medical care, of course, but prayer? Prayer is hope and love."

"Can we get the check?" I asked our server.

CHAPTER 23

THERE WILL BE LOBSTER

"I would love that," I said to my son when he called to say he wanted to come home from Utah with a bunch of friends for New Year's Eve. I didn't want to end up in a Mexican restaurant like I had the previous year, drinking pitchers of margaritas with hungover revelers still wearing their 2014 glasses from the night before. *This is it*, I thought. *New year, new hope*. It had been two years since my daughter left for college. It had been two years of me searching, seeking, and feeling lost and alone. *This is just what I need*, I told myself, *to come back to life*. My daughter could return from college to a place that would feel like a home again. She could bring her boyfriend too. It would be a great start. A fresh start. I would make things right. Nice. Normal.

"I'll make a big New Year's Day brunch at the house for everyone," I told him.

"I don't have any plans for New Year's Eve, as usual, so I can get everything organized."

I thought about how I'd behaved when I went to visit him in Utah a couple months prior for Thanksgiving, when I finally had the nerve to go back after my birthday debacle. He still talks about how he found me passed out on his bed that Thanksgiving Day after simultaneously chugging two bottles of wine in a move called "the walrus." *I have to redeem myself*, I thought. *I can't strike out a third time. I can be a better, more nurturing Mom and feel good about myself again. This is the perfect way to start things out.* The new year would usher in life-affirming redemption. I could put all my sadness behind. I could stop wallowing around in the mud, searching for answers I already had, and reenter the world as a positive and productive human being. I could take off my sweatpants and put on a dress—something celebratory, with sparkles. It had been a difficult two years. I'd lost my business, and I'd lost my self-worth. But it was time I stopped hurting myself and those I loved and looked to the future.

My now-legendary walrus episode all began as a joke. My son was in his third year of college at the University of Utah. We were in his off-campus apartment in Salt Lake City, which looked every bit like the off-campus apartment of a bunch of twenty-somethings (empty beer bottles, unwashed dishes, strange odors rising from the carpets), and my son was playfully coaxing me on. He was probably waiting for me to say, "No way. I'm not going there again!" But I was determined to show him I could still do anything. I was still up for everything.

"Mom. Do the walrus," my son urged as we all sat around the Thanksgiving dinner table, which was actually four folding tables positioned haphazardly across the living room.

"Yeah," said a dozen of his college friends in unison. "Do the walrus!"

To everyone's surprise, I picked up two bottles of wine, shoved both of them in my mouth to look like tusks, then tipped my head back to chug as much as possible. The red wine dribbled out of my mouth and ran down the front of my shirt. Everyone cheered wildly. I sat upright and removed the bottles, handing them to the kid next to me who proceeded to chug them without spilling a drop. *What a pro*, I thought.

I had decided to spend the holiday with my son in Salt Lake City. I made two trays of macaroni and cheese a few days before I left so I could freeze them to pack in my luggage. I had packed more food than clothes. I felt relieved about not having to host a big Thanksgiving dinner. I was happy that there was no fireplace to tend to, happy there were no aromas of scented candles and potpourri or decorations that heralded the holiday season to come. The only festive decoration at his house was the stuffed deer head over the front door. It had lights on its antlers and a cigarette poking out of its mouth. I was fairly sure this was there year-round.

The lack of tablecloths, linen napkins, and polished silverware were a great relief. I didn't have to make small talk. I didn't have to pretend that I was excited that the turkey turned the perfect shade of brown from the red-wine-soaked cheese cloth I had draped over it while roasting. There were no guests I wished I hadn't had to invite. There wasn't even a turkey. There was something else that looked like the science project version of a turkey—boneless layers of poultry meat molded together and pinned into a turkey-like shape. The tables were plastic. The chairs didn't match. The plates were paper. And I did the walrus.

"I love you," I said to my son, across the room. "I'm so glad to be here with you and your friends."

"Are you OK, Mom?"

He stopped me before I could say another word. He sounded worried.

"Yeah. Why?"

"I don't know. Don't get weird. Get some more food."

"I'm going to," I said, and took my paper plate to the kitchen for more.

A vegan girl stood at the stove cooking Brussels sprouts for herself.

The guy who brought the turkey-like creation was basting it in the oven.

Someone was opening beers with their teeth.

The dog was eating food that had been dropped on the floor.

Someone grabbed a skateboard and started doing tricks on the back patio.

I picked a twice-baked potato from an aluminum baking pan and placed it on my plate.

"I made those," one of my son's friends said to me.

"Oh wow, it looks so good," I complimented.

"Are you OK?" he asked.

"Yeah. Great." I was annoyed at this question.

"Well, let me know if you need anything. I know where everything is here. I'm sure this isn't the type of Thanksgiving you're used to."

No one ever understood that I wasn't above most things and could get used to almost any situation I found myself in. I was not on a pedestal and had no illusions of superiority. I had faith in my self-sufficiency, but somehow it seemed to manifest as detachment. Disdain. Aloofness. Caution. Fear. In actuality, I didn't care whether I used a paper plate or fine china. I was happy to be out of my house, letting others do all the work of Thanksgiving. I didn't care at that moment about a roaring fire, flowers on the table, pies on pie stands waiting to be cut and served, or asking people if they wanted tea or coffee with dessert. I didn't care if I ate with my fingers, wiped my hands on my pants, and let the red wine stain on my shirt just dry there.

So why did I feel like every five minutes someone was asking me if I was OK? What did my face look like? What expression was I wearing that seemed to cause worry? I didn't like the feeling that people thought I needed looking after, that I needed to be checked up on as if I was going to dash into the road in front of a car when not supervised.

"Let's do the walrus again," I yelled out to set things right and even the field. But no one wanted to. They looked at me like I might suddenly implode. The rest of the visit was polite conversation. Even my son, who always likes to tease me, treated me with soft words and small talk. And I hated myself for it.

"I love that you're coming home for New Year's," I now told my son. "This will be fun. I'll make all your favorite things for New Year's Day. We'll have a big, delicious brunch with a ton of food. I'll be up early to get everything ready. I'll get fresh lobster. I'll buy a dozen and we can cook them and eat them warm from their shells with drawn butter. This will be a real celebration. A great start to 2015. I can't wait."

CHAPTER 24

JUST BREATHE

I walked into the large, open loft in New York's SoHo neighborhood. It was an all-white photo studio set up with a combination of folding chairs and meditation chairs, which looked like floor cushions with backs. I chose the regular chair. I didn't want to be on the floor. It felt restrictive. It felt like it would be too hard to stand up and flee if I suddenly felt anxious. A chair, I thought, was easier to get up from for a faster, quieter escape. This was how I had started seeing the world. I always needed an escape route. I was always afraid. My preparation rituals were less about being ready or successful and more about abandonment and evacuation. *What if I see someone I know*, I thought, *someone who hasn't seen me with this much weight on my bones, someone who watches me struggle to lift myself from the floor cushion, someone who gives me either one of two looks I dread—the "poor you" face or the "fuck you" face.* Either was possible, and neither was something I could handle. *Aw c'mon*, I told myself. *You can get up from the floor; it's not that bad yet.* I tried to get the motivation to sit there, tried to convince myself to step outside of the box I had walled myself within. But I didn't believe in myself enough to choose a floor cushion over a chair. I stuck with the idea that sitting in a folding chair was better. Less hazardous. More in control.

I picked one in the back row, near the elevator. *If I feel overcome with anxiety, or worry, or paranoia,* I thought, *I can disappear with almost no notice. One step at a time. At least you're here. At least you're not sitting in a pool of your own regurgitation and regret.* I flashed back to the lobster crawling out from under the kitchen chair on New Year's Day. I remembered the mess in the kitchen and the mess I had become. I touched my cheek that had been swollen and black from hitting my head against the toilet. A few months had passed since then. My daughter was finally speaking to me again. I knew I had to do something to really help myself. I knew that I had to be like the surviving lobster and crawl into the open to be saved.

We were crammed in, side by side, all looking ahead at a table covered with a white cloth and several accessories: small brass bowls filled with spices, a small bowl with water, and a candle. I looked down at the people on the floor and was happy I got there early enough to get a chair. We were told to each bring a bunch of flowers and a few pieces of washed fruit. I placed my deli bouquet of mixed flowers and an apple and an orange on the floor next to my chair. Tonight, I was going to get my mantra and become a fully initiated Vedic meditator. My guru said that he was considered the number-one mantra-giver. I felt confident that I was at the right place with the right guy. It was funny to think I now had a guru. I wondered if it was pretentious. "Hey, of course I have a guru. Don't you?" I imagined myself saying without any hint of humor.

When my office closed, I joined a shared workspace in NYC—a membership-only place where I could hang out and feign that I had something to do. On one of my visits there for the free 5:00 p.m. happy hour, I saw a young woman sitting on a cushion in the window with her eyes closed. "She's meditating," someone said to me as he saw me staring. "She manages a famous meditation teacher, a top guru," he said and offered to introduce me. He said they were good friends. I told him I'd just finished an online meditation course and thanked him. He pressed on, saying that I should meet her anyway because her guru was the best and that I could learn a lot with him and take my practice to the next level.

I had just finished Deepak Chopra and Oprah's 21-Day Meditation Experience online. In my search for psychic healing, I had missed meditation as a practice that could help me until I had a drink one afternoon with an old friend that I hadn't seen in a while. He was mindlessly snapping a thin, red rubber band that he had on his wrist while he looked me in the eye and told me what was happening in his life. I couldn't stop looking at the small welt that was forming on his arm. He saw me frown.

"It keeps me mindful."

"Doesn't it hurt?"

"I don't snap it that hard."

"I can see a red mark."

"I'm going to take it off soon. I did a twenty-one day meditation challenge. You should do it. I did it with Deepak Chopra and Oprah."

"Wow. How did you get into that class?"

"It's online. Anyone can do it."

"Oh. And it works?"

"It's great. I don't really need the rubber band anymore. It's just habit now."

So I did it. I logged on and listened to the voices of Deepak and Oprah tell me to breathe, to relax, to close my eyes and think about mindfulness, or abundance, or other topics they covered during our twenty-one days together on my laptop. I didn't want to have to snap myself into mindfulness. I didn't want pain to be what kept me alert and attentive. I wanted something more peaceful to ground me, and the lulling voices of two of the world's most famous people did the trick. When I completed the 21-Day Meditation Experience with Deepak and Oprah, my daughter said I sounded different when we talked on the phone. She said I seemed calmer than the last few times we'd spoken. She said she was happy I stuck with it. She said it was the first thing I didn't give up on in a while. Like the scarves I stopped knitting or the plants I stopped tending or the closets I didn't finish organizing and on and on. She said she was proud of me. I wondered if the universe was shifting and a gathering storm of cosmic dust was organizing itself in order to whisk me into a new world and a new way of being.

"I'm good," I told her. "I actually am calmer than I've been in a while, although I still have my moments. I read that if you meditate forty minutes a day for eight weeks, you can reprogram your brain and exist in a permanent blissed-out state where nothing will ever get to you, bother you, or scare you again." I told her that although I didn't think this was actually the case, I was going to keep meditating anyway.

"Good for you," she said. "I'm glad."

The guru began his talk. He sat with one leg tucked under him on a bench or some type of raised platform. He talked about stress and how we, as almost newly initiated Vedic meditators, now had the power to deal with it, to make it go away. He told us that we could learn to breathe so deeply that we disconnect our sympathetic nervous system and separate what we feel in our mind from what we feel in our body. He talked about how we're all born with a fight-or-flight response. Our nervous system unleashes a cascade of hormones when we feel threatened or highly stressed.

Blood vessels restrict.

The heart beats faster.

Palms sweat.

You want to run.

You want to get the fuck away from whatever's making you feel like this.

You want your stomach to stop turning over and over.

You want to scream.

The guru said that the solution is to stay and play.

Stay and play.

Stay and play, I repeated to myself over and over.

Yes, I thought. *I'm a fighter or a flighter.* I fight with my own demons. I binge on wine thinking they'll go away for a little while and give me some peace, but when I wake up with my head pounding and the bags under my eyes twice the size they should be, I realize the demons are right where I left them, there, on my shoulder, challenging me to fight them off or run from them. I wanted to stay and play. I wanted to be able to face things again and, most critically, face myself.

Stay and play. *Yes*, I said to myself. I felt clarity like I hadn't in a while. Plans formed in my head for a future I could be proud of. I looked around at the people in the room. *These could be my new friends*, I thought. I was excited to get my mantra.

I'm going to get my mantra, I told myself.

I'm going to chant my mantra.

I'm going to be maniacal about making the time to meditate every day, twice a day.

I'm going to take better care of myself—eat better, love myself better, respect myself more.

I'm going to slow down my heartbeat and resist my hormonal urges to flee from situations that make me feel uncomfortable, insecure, and diminished.

I'm going to trust myself again, and next time I come to a meditation session, I'm going to sit on a floor cushion because I won't want to run. I won't feel the need to take flight.

The guru finished up his talk by leading us in a twenty-minute group meditation.

"Wow," I said to the person sitting next to me after we wiggled our toes, opened our eyes, and emerged from the meditative state.

"Yeah," she said.

I wondered what I would have found if it wasn't meditation.

Would I be sitting at a bar sipping a glass of rosé, pretending I was not drinking alone, pretending I was waiting for someone who was running late, then, three glasses later, telling the bartender plans changed and that "he" wasn't coming anymore and could I have the check? Or similarly, would I strike up a conversation with someone at the bar and commiserate together about being stood up, left out, and drinking alone through no fault of our own? Would I toast with him or her to evicting inconsiderate assholes from our lives, order another drink, and sit like a reconciled bar fly who has just landed on a pile of fresh shit?

Would I be wandering around my house never bothering to get dressed and not caring about anything more than wanting the day to turn to night as quickly as possible? Wondering how early was too early for me to crawl into bed for the night? 6:30? 7:00?

Would I take up whistling or humming to break the silence of having no one to talk to?

Would I wear a rubber band on my wrist and snap myself into life until the swelling itself became its own painful reminder that I needed resuscitation?

If I didn't find meditation, would closing my eyes continue to haunt me with thoughts of tragedy and death? I saw them all the time. I worried about them all the time. I had to yell at myself to stop it when I shut my eyes and saw my daughter lying dead in a field.

Lying dead in the road.

Lying dead in a bed.

Lying dead in my arms.

Maybe now, maybe soon, I can close my eyes, I thought, *and see a flower. A butterfly. The smiling face of my daughter. See beauty. See a future for myself.*

It was time to get our mantras. A line formed. The guru sat on one of the folding chairs at the end of the studio. There was another folding chair, facing him. The newly initiated walked up to the guru one by one and sat in front of him. When it was my turn, I walked toward him slowly. It felt like a procession. "Pomp and Circumstance" was playing in my head. He smelled like sandalwood and incense. I breathed him in and exhaled the hope of something better. The fruit and flowers from the ceremony were piled high on the white table. He said we could take some on our way out. I walked to the chair positioned next to him. I felt wobbly. *What if I fall on him?* I thought. *What if I stumble?* I was so unsure of myself in every way. My lack of comfort with my body—with my entire being—made me think I had no more motor skills than a waddling toddler. I sat down without issue, putting my exaggerated worries behind, and breathed a sigh of relief. He smiled. I think I did the same. He told me to lean forward and, with his face to my ear, whispered my mantra. He repeated it three times then asked me to whisper it back to him. "Good," he said. "It's yours. Don't give it to anyone else because it won't work for them."

"Thank you," I said, then got up and left. I took a bite of the apple I picked up from the table as I walked out.

I missed Oprah and Deepak. I missed being talked through twenty minutes of meditating. *I still need guidance*, I thought. The guru told me that thoughts would come into my head when I was meditating. He said I could get frustrated and feel like it's not working. He said if this happened to focus on the mantra and that all these random and extraneous thoughts would float away. I didn't like to be alone with my thoughts. When I closed my eyes, I still saw things I didn't want to see. I thought things I didn't want to contemplate. Meditation didn't make these go away. I remembered things I pushed back in my mind. *I pushed them back for a reason*, I thought. I pushed them back because they were too painful to deal with. Being alone with my thoughts dredged up memories. Scenes played back in my mind of situations and events and words and actions I hadn't thought about in years. Sometimes I cried uncontrollably, and the calm of meditating was shattered by my breathy sobs.

I wondered where these painful memories and repressed emotions were hiding in my body when they weren't emerging to remind me that I didn't deserve peace or happiness. Were they tucked under one of my fleshy folds? Did they have shapes? What color were they? Why was I now crying about some jerk from high school that made me feel bad? I thought I had overcome so much of what was coming back during meditation. "If they're there," said my guru, "you have to deal with them. Sit with your feelings, even for a moment, and don't push them away."

"This is the work of meditation," he said.

"These are stressors that need to be released," he said.

"Don't give up," he said.

My mind worked overtime during meditation. It dredged up things I obviously had not reconciled and released from my large suitcase of emotional baggage. It brought back memories, mostly painful, that needed to be released. It also brought back memories that needed to be reevaluated and re-stored with a more realistic perspective. I needed to rid myself of the negativity I had accumulated in my memory banks. *They are coloring how I see things today. I need a memory makeover*, I said to myself. I realized I needed to see things through a more positive lens when I remembered a phone call from André Leon Talley, the legendary fashion editor. He was in the back seat of a car service, driving up Madison Avenue. I'd known André since I helped answer his phone as a young assistant at *Vanity Fair* magazine.

"I'm following your ex. I'm in a car service. He's walking up Madison Avenue. He's wearing pants that have been tailored. You can tell they've been fitted by a very good tailor. But his feet look like they hurt. His shoes look tight. His feet are pinched. The shoes are very narrow. He's walking slowly. His feet are killing him. I can tell. He's with a woman." He said he had to go because he was holding up traffic, and he had a meeting at the Sant Ambroeus restaurant a few blocks away.

I need to let this go, I thought, *and focus on the mantra. I need to do what I was taught to do—let the thoughts that come into my head during meditation leave my body and float away. I'm getting rid of clutter.*

I was glad that meditation would help me take the stress reaction from this memory and let me revisit it in the way it was meant to be received. It was funny. It was silly. It was André being a friend to me, as always. It was André being André and reaching out to let me know, in his own way, that he was thinking of me. I brought myself back to my mantra again and finished meditating. When I opened my eyes, I felt calm. I was OK, I realized. I was smiling at the thought of André scrunched down in the back seat of a car, spying from a distance. I imagined him in his signature caftan, phone in hand, peering out the back window, reporting on a fashion scene. *I'm good*, I thought. *I can stay and play with my own thoughts.*

Memories kept bubbling up. I thought about a phone call I got from a shoe store I used to frequent. I tried not to think of this moment and always pushed it away when it surfaced. It made me angry and upset. It was a memory that I wanted to see through a new, more positive lens, so I assumed this is why it was dredged up during meditation. I played back the call from a salesperson telling me the shoes I ordered were in. I told him that I hadn't ordered any shoes. "Hold on, please," he said.

A manager I knew for a long time from shopping there picked up the phone. "Hello darling," he said. "Well, I guess you can figure out what happened just now; we called the wrong 'Mrs.'"

"Yes," I said, knowing that I hadn't been there in a long time and didn't buy any shoes.

"Now you know," he said. "We miss you. Come visit."

"I will," I said. I thanked him, not sure for what. I ended the call and burst into tears. I couldn't get control of my emotions. I couldn't even articulate what I was crying about. Was it the fact that I was not the one buying multiple pairs of expensive shoes? "Now you know," he'd said. *Know what?* I thought. All I knew was that I wasn't in control of my reactions and was bouncing around emotionally like a spinning top. Why didn't I laugh when I realized it wasn't me they should have called and said something to diffuse the awkward moment and rise above a simple mistake? I had lost all perspective. Why didn't I say something like, "Hey, are they my size?" and laugh it away? I could have joked back, eased the discomfort we all felt. But all I could do was put down my phone and cry. Again. Blurt out in self-pity. Again. I went back to my mantra and finished my twenty minutes, which felt more like a painful past-life regression than an ancient Vedic practice designed to help combat stress and generate inner peace. *Keep going, I told myself. Don't give up. Meditation's been around for a long time. It's gotta work, because I've got nothing else.*

I need coffee NOW, I told myself one morning. Typically, I sat up in bed and meditated before I even went downstairs. I would wake up, go to the bathroom, prop up my pillows, sit up in bed, and start my morning meditation. I always had ups and downs with getting started and settling in. Beginning was the hardest part. I frequently checked the clock to see how much time had passed. Sometimes it was only a few minutes when it seemed like more. I realized multiple times during my meditation that I lost my mantra and was ticking off the shopping list. I daydreamed. Things came into my head that I had hoped never to think of again. There were times when I just opened my eyes as if I forgot I was meditating. And there were the mornings when I would power through my meditation for twenty minutes, ignoring my instruction to be easy and almost lazy with the mantra. I would silently chant my syllabic sounds in a fast, unrelenting breath where I'd breathe in on the first sound and out on the second. There were many mornings when I wanted to give up because it seemed too hard to focus for twenty minutes, the way I was taught.

"We don't try to meditate," I was told.

"Mantra is a vague, faint idea," I was reminded.

"Let the mantra float away. You don't even have to enunciate it," I was told.

"Be effortless with the mantra," I was ultimately instructed.

121

But this one morning, my head was bobbing, and my chin was on my chest. I couldn't keep my eyes open or my mind alert. My mantra disappeared from my thoughts and I couldn't get it back. *I can't. I need coffee now. Coffee won't interfere with my state of readiness for meditation, and it certainly won't make me tired. This isn't working,* I complained to myself. *It's actually stressing me out.* I felt my brow furrow and my jaw clench.

I threw back the covers to get out of bed and head to the kitchen. *If I just had coffee, I could get back to it. And maybe just a little something to eat as well,* I concluded as my stomach growled back at me. I sat on the edge of the bed, about to get up, when I saw a bird fly into my window. It lightly hit the glass then disappeared out of sight to the patio below. I threw open the window and looked down. The bird wasn't dead. It hopped around on the stone floor as it recovered from this mishap. *It's just a little stunned,* I thought. I kept watching, wanting to make sure the bird would be OK. After a few minutes, the bird flew into the cherry tree outside my window and sat on a branch facing me. We looked at each other. *I'm making eye contact with this bird,* I thought.

I wondered if it was a sign that things would be all right. I thought of the dove that Noah sent from the ark after the rains stopped to see if the waters had receded and dry land was emerging. Noah knew that the dove would come back to the ark if it couldn't find a dry place to settle. When the dove returned to the ark, Noah knew that the world was still covered with water. Seven days later, he sent the dove out again. He waited seven more days, and when the dove didn't return, he knew that the waters had subsided, and the dove had found a place to land. The bird in the cherry tree took flight after a few more moments and disappeared onto the distance. *Was this my "ark moment"?* I thought. *Was this bird letting me know that the world was a safe place for me again and that I could begin to reestablish myself? Was this experience telling me that we all hit obstacles but need to overcome them and continue on? That we need to find a place to alight and begin walking the land again*? I closed the window and went right back to bed. I was always looking for signs and signals and couldn't help but believe this was a big one. It seemed to me that I had a biblical lesson play out before my eyes. *If you can't pay attention to this*, I told myself, *you are completely underwater*. I knew that coffee and food and all my other self-indulgent needs of the moment could wait, and I finished meditating.

CHAPTER 25

I WANT TO COME HOME

"I want to come home," my daughter said. "I want to transfer to a school close to home."

"Why?" I asked, trying to sound neutral and caring when all I wanted to say was "Pack now, I'm on my way."

"It's not good for me here anymore," she said. "It's just not right for me anymore."

I had waited for this day for two years, longed for it. I didn't even care if she wanted to drop out of college and take a break, as long as she was coming home. I dreamed of having her back in her room, the two of us sitting at the kitchen table together in the morning, quietly preparing for the day, her scent and presence filling the air. I was looking forward to finding a cold, half-consumed cup of coffee on a side table or counter. Signs of her. Habits of her. When she told me that she wanted to transfer to a college near home and commute, I wanted to do cartwheels across the kitchen floor. *Nothing would make me happier*, I thought. Then my self-sabotage mechanism kicked in.

"You know I'm selling the house," I reminded her. "I don't have a plan as to where I'll live or what I'll do. I was counting on you being away at school while I figured things out. If you come home,

I don't know if I'll even have room for you, wherever I end up. I was actually thinking of finding some small cabin on a lake, somewhere kind of remote. I can't really do that if you come home and want to commute to a school. I don't know. Are you really sure?" I asked. "Are you really sure you want to come home? I thought you might even stay in Vermont after school finished for the semester. I kind of counted on that too. That apartment you had last summer over the bar looked nice."

I suddenly felt like I was stuck to the couch. There was a heaviness that washed over me, and I couldn't move. I felt disconnected to the reprehensible words that came out of my mouth:

"This is taking me by surprise."

"I have to think about this."

"I'm not sure this will work."

"Can't you just figure it out?"

I could see myself wriggle and squirm while I talked on the phone and told my daughter she wasn't welcome, that the timing was wrong, that there wasn't any room. I watched myself hold my arm to the side with the phone away from my face so she couldn't hear me crying. My nose was running, and tears streamed down my cheeks.

Stop it, I commanded myself.

Get it together.

Be a mom for her.

Stop denying what you want.

See yourself as worthy of being happy.

Cut the crap.

Cut the shit.

Come back, I pleaded with the part of myself that seemed to have disassociated from my body to watch me with disgust from across the room. *Come back*, I said to my conscience. *I need you. Breathe. Breathe through this and get it together.*

"I'm coming home at the end of the term, Mom," she said calmly.

"OK," I answered.

"I'm glad," I finally said, exhaling loudly.

"I'm really glad. We'll figure it out."

I wanted to change a few small things and perk up the house for her. I bought a photo by Slim Aarons called *Poolside Gossip* and decided to hang it over the fireplace in my bedroom. I moved the artwork that had been hanging there for years. It depicted the death of Socrates. I don't know why it took me so long to move this death scene. Maybe it was self-punishment. The painting showed the philosopher in his room, surrounded by bereft followers as he was preparing to drink poison and die. *It's time finally*, I thought. *I can stop relating to this image. It's not me.* I took it off the wall. I wanted to see life, not death. I wanted to rid myself of negative influences. I wanted to be surrounded instead by positive premonitions. I wanted to wake up and look at the scene Aarons photographed—a white, modernist house in Palm Springs, California, with beautiful people sitting around a clear, blue pool. I imagined that the two stylish women sitting in lounge chairs at the end of the long pool could be me and a friend. The house was simple and elegant. It was surrounded by lush greenery and sat in front of a backdrop of majestic blue-and-purple-hued mountains.

"This could be my dream house," I told my daughter as we were sitting in my bed together looking at it on the wall, both happy that she was back home.

"I'm so glad you moved that painting. It was depressing."

"I know," I said. "I don't know why it took so long to realize that I shouldn't be staring at a death scene upon waking. But this feels like possibility. It feels like something to look forward to—a simple, uncomplicated existence—one that's easy to live and live within. I feel like selling all my possessions and starting again. I want to unclutter. I want clean surfaces, no knickknacks, and I want a uniform. I want to dress the same way every day. People do this," I told her. There were fashion editors that did this to make their busy lives a little bit easier. "You wore a uniform all throughout middle school," I reminded her.

"I just want to be happy," I continued. "Stuff doesn't make me happy anymore. It used to once. It used to validate my being. I bought things I didn't even want or need just to know that I could. But they weren't inspiring. They served no purpose in my happiness. Someone I knew a long time ago remembered that I had a diamond necklace—a really expensive one—and asked if he could buy it from me for his girlfriend. I told him that I had only worn it once in all the years I had it and that I would be willing to sell it to him. It didn't mean anything to me. It never had, I realized. Then he said he would give me half of its value because it was secondhand jewelry. I couldn't believe it. What a scam. So, of course, I didn't follow through because I didn't want to get ripped off, but it made me think that having too much, having more than you need, is a burden in so many ways, and I don't want to live that life anymore. I want things that inspire me."

CHAPTER 26

TURN LEFT

I found a small, nondescript rental house that we could live in for a year while I looked for a new home—a first home for the new, new me. The me that meditated every day, twice a day. The me that was not rampantly and meaninglessly consuming material possessions. The me that washed and got dressed, at least on most days. The me that was digging out of the deep dark hole that I had resided in for two years. The me that had my younger daughter back home, going to a nearby college as a day student. The me that wanted a fresh start in a new home where I could make the memories that would sustain me as I moved forward. *The portal that was sucking me into blackness is closing,* I thought. I was on the other side of it, in the light.

"I'm running to the store," I told my daughter one weekend afternoon while we were packing to move to the rental. "I'll be back soon."

I thought about how much I liked driving down roads I knew intimately and the comfort that came with living in the same place for close to twenty years. I dodged the pothole at the end of the driveway, bypassed the rock that stuck into the road too much, and shook my head in disappointment at the trees that were planted too close together and dying at the bottom where the sun couldn't reach the branches. I smiled at the cairn—the pile of rocks that someone had built on the lawn, next to the driveway entrance. I let it stand and wondered if the new owner would too. I considered the idea of leaving a piece of me behind, something that would be secretly lingering, lurking, and holding my place here. Then I remembered that I had recently buried a small statue in the yard.

"My house is for sale," I told my psychic during one of my continuing readings.

"Take this," she said. "It's a statue of St. Joseph. Bury it in your front yard, upside down, facing your house. Then say a prayer."

"What kind of prayer?"

"To St. Joseph, you know. Something like 'Saint Joseph, I want to sell this house quickly; please help me.' You might as well also sprinkle a line of salt around the house to keep out negativity. It can't hurt."

I threw the groceries in the back of the car and headed home. I turned off the highway onto the narrow dirt road—my road. I navigated like I was on autopilot. I knew where every ditch, hole, and bump resided. I swerved with complete confidence. *I'll miss this road*, I thought. *It's right out of a picture book that could be entitled*, Quaint Country Roads. When I came to the stop sign at the end, I looked both ways to make sure there weren't any cars coming before I took the right up a hill that led to my house. Or, more accurately, my soon-to-be-former house. In front of me, stuck in the ground on the opposite side of the road, was an "Open House" sign for another house that was for sale, with an arrow pointing the way—the way I didn't usually go.

I turned left.

"I can't believe it," I said aloud to myself.

A version of the *Poolside Gossip* house—the title of the Aarons photo that now lived in my bedroom—loomed in front of me. It was slightly different than the house in the photograph, of course, but similar enough for it to be a sign—white, modern, and sleek. Even the "Open House" sign was a sign, I thought. A sign that appeared right in front of me that told me to turn left instead of right. A sign that pointed out a different path. A sign that had never been there before any of the hundreds of times I'd driven home and that showed itself when I needed it most. "Thank you," I said aloud, to put my gratitude into the world.

I believed for the first time in a long time that the universe was talking to me:

Hey, don't live in the past. It's over.

Follow the sign.

Come up this driveway. See something new.

You made this happen. You have to believe.

Left is the new right.

I know my life isn't rooted in walls and things and rooms that are empty, I thought. *This was meant to be.* I'd passed this driveway hundreds of times without any interest. I had never even considered what was hidden at the top of the hill.

I cringed at the memory of that New Year's Day in my bathroom. I relived it almost every time I used the toilet. The stain was still on the floor, etched into the white, marble tile. It was impermeable to every cleaning solution and YouTube hack. Nothing could penetrate that night to make it disappear. The shadow of my vomit screamed at me. Every time I looked down at the floor, it looked up at me.

You're a fuckup, it said.

You're a fat mess, it said.

Act like a mom.

Get a job.

Go back to work.

Move on.

Earn the respect of your children again.

Shower.

Dress.

Fucking do something.

"I'm going in," I said to myself and walked to the front door, which seemed to me like an entryway to a new world, one that had been beckoning to me for a long time.

"Hey," I said to the realtor who was sitting at the kitchen counter.

It was December 2016. My home was sold and I moved into a rental house, which was isolated down a long driveway out of view of neighbors whose homes were similarly isolated. A handyman who worked for the owners sometimes emerged from the woods to see if I needed anything, reminding me that there was life nearby. The main bedroom was on the first floor, next to the front door and down a short hall from the kitchen. I liked that I could stay in bed and see or hear everything that was going on in the house. I bought an artificial, pre-lit Christmas tree from Amazon and put it in the front hallway next to my bedroom. *Happy holidays*, I said to myself. *This is home for now.*

"New year, new chance," I said aloud as I plugged in my fake tree and thought about real life and what this new year would bring.

"I like this house," my daughter said one day when she came home from her classes at the nearby college she was now attending.

"Yeah. It feels good, mostly because you're here," I said, "but also because it's the start of something new for us. It's inspiring, in a weird way. The house is a bit of a wreck and none of our furniture fits, but somehow it all hangs together. It's good enough for now." I shifted into a more positive tone. "I'm good," I assured her. "Really good. I'm getting ready to take off my sweatpants, no joke. I'm seeing a doctor to help me lose this weight. I'm finally taking control of things." I turned on the gas fireplace in the kitchen with the click of a switch and settled down in front of it to keep talking with my daughter as she made herself something to eat.

"I saw your sign," I said to the realtor who was in the kitchen of the white, modern house at the top of the hill.

"Welcome," she said, handing me a brochure. "Have a look around. It's a very unique house for this area. It's all in the folder. Read it."

The white brick house was constructed as two circles sitting on top of each other. *Circles*, I thought, *like the moon and the sun.*

A cocoon.

A womb.

A wheel.

A curve.

I couldn't wait to walk around.

I manifested this house, I wanted to tell her.

I see a modern house, almost like this, every morning when I wake up. It's fate that brought me here.

I should have taken a right, but I went left for the first time in all the years I've lived here.

This has to mean something, I wanted to say.

Circles are spiritual. They're safe places. They envelop you within their walls and keep you wrapped in their energy. God is a circle.

"Does it have a pool?" I asked.

"It's across the driveway," she said.

I walked to the pool so I could picture myself on a lounge chair looking across the blue water like the ladies in the Aarons photo, then walked back to the house. *Yes*, I thought. *I can see myself here.*

"Do you have any offers?" I asked.

"People think it needs a lot of work. Also, it's not the house people tend to want up here. They're mostly looking for a farmhouse style or a center-hall colonial."

A couple walked in while I was talking to the realtor. "We love modern houses," they said. "Can you tell us about this one?"

"Sure," the realtor said and excused herself from me.

They must look like serious buyers, I thought. *She stood up when they walked in.* I could see her gesticulating and pointing as she walked away and left me in the kitchen. I wished I had worn real pants and not my baggy old sweats.

"I think it's perfect," I said to the realtor and the couple on my way out. "I love it. I'm going to buy this house. I'm in a rental now, so

I'll have the time to fix it up," I yelled over my shoulder, confirming my seriousness.

The couple smiled. "You should," they said. "It's amazing. It needs too much work for us."

CHAPTER 27

IT'S JUST A COLD

I landed in Los Angeles to visit my older daughter, who had relocated there from the Bay Area. She picked me up at the airport and told me I looked like shit and asked why I didn't tell her I was sick before I got on a plane. I said I had a little cold that I couldn't shake, but it would be fine. I felt sorry for the people sitting next to me. I squirted Afrin up my nose relentlessly and went through a box of tissues. I also consumed an entire family-size bag of Ricola cough drops to try to control the hacking cough that had roused more disgusted looks and comments than I'd had the energy to respond to.

"I don't think I'm contagious anymore," I said to the woman sitting next to me on the plane. "Don't worry."

"Sick people shouldn't travel," someone nearby said aloud for my benefit.

"Sorry," I said.

My daughter took me straight to an urgent care center in Brentwood. She picked Brentwood, she said, because it was a nice part of Los Angeles and most people there probably had their own doctors, so it might not be too crowded. She was right. It was empty, and the doctor saw me right away. I left with an inhaler and a Z-Pak. The doctor suggested I get a chest X-ray. I told her I didn't have time.

"Ridiculous," my older daughter said as we drove to her house.

"It's just a little cold."

"Have you seen yourself? And all you do is cough. You have to see your doctor when you get home. And get that chest X-ray."

I had moved into the rental house during the first snowstorm of the season in early December. The storm was unexpected. The snow began the minute the moving trucks arrived and didn't let up the entire day. The house was freezing from the doors being propped open, and I was cold and wet from running back and forth, inside and outside, grabbing boxes and organizing where things needed to be placed for unpacking. *That is when I got sick*, I thought. *It's how I got the cold from hell that I just can't shake.*

"I got this cold when I moved to the rental house," I told my older daughter. "It snowed the entire day I moved in. I got a chill. I need to rest. I finally can, now that I'm all unpacked. It took me months to get organized. I just didn't have the energy. But I'm here now. I missed you and couldn't wait any longer for a visit. Maybe we can sit on the beach in the sun a bit," I said. "The sun is so healing. It might help dry me up."

"I hate the sun," she said. "It causes skin cancer. You need to stay in bed. Besides, the move was three months ago. No one has a cold for three months and does nothing about it."

"I know," I said. "But the good news is that I bought a new house that I'm going to dive into fixing up when I feel better. It needs a lot of work, but it will be great. I really love it."

"Was it hard to sell the old house?" she asked, remembering that my life had recently been uprooted, remembering, maybe, that I had caught this cold during a stressful period of upheaval and change.

"No," I answered. "It was time."

"I get it," she said.

"Yep," I said.

"You better see your regular doctor—not your chiropractor or some other quack you found as soon as you get home," she repeated.

"We can still have fun," I said.

The doctor that I was seeing for weight loss called me and asked if I'd been fighting off a cold or infection of some sort.

"Yes," I said, "I had a cold that was hard to shake."

"Yes," I said, "I just got back from LA and was sick the whole time."

"Yes," I said, "I've been fighting it off for months."

She said my white blood cell count was a bit high so I should come back in when I had time to get it re-checked, but not to worry; it was most likely from the lingering cold. I put it out of my mind and carried on with life. I was ready to shed the pounds I had gained. I wanted to button my pants and tuck in my shirt again. I wanted to be able to hold a plank at the gym without crumbling into a crying mess. I wanted to walk down the street and be able to make eye contact with people instead of hiding because I felt so bad about the lumpy mess I had let myself become. I wanted to be able to honestly answer the question "How are you?" with optimism, sincerity, and truthfulness.

"Fine" wasn't cutting it for me anymore.

"Great" was a lie.

"Eh, you know" was a cop-out.

The doctor was thorough. She drew blood to check for vitamin deficiencies and allergies. She told me to cut out all dairy and not to eat bananas. She said I was allergic to bananas.

"I knew I didn't like them for a reason," I said.

"Listen to your body," she said.

She told me that I was the hardest kind of patient to treat because I never complained when I didn't feel well.

"You suck it up, but you need to be honest about how you feel because we can help you feel better. You don't have to power through things. If you tell me how you're responding to the diet I'm putting you on, we can adjust it so that it works for you," she said.

"I want you to feel good."

"I do too," I told her.

"I'm going to give you supplements to take and a protein shake. You need protein and to work out. You need to build muscle and decrease your BMI. We'll get you there," she said.

"OK," I sighed.

Back home, I quietly listened to the sound of my breath as I settled in to meditate. I chanted my mantra silently and lazily as my guru instructed. When I opened my eyes, I stared ahead.

I tried to feel nothing.

I tried to forget how I got to this place in my life.

I tried to forget my fears.

I tried to focus on my hopes.

I saw a piece of dust on the floor. I watched it dance on the air being pushed up through the floor vents. The breath of the house was moving it around, having its way with the dust. It moved up and down, back and forth. The air stopped blowing, and the dust settled back on the floor. *That's me*, I thought. *I'm like a piece of dust that's moved by a force beyond its control.* I liked the idea of being driven by a breeze. *Good things come in on a breeze. I still need to pay attention to things that move in front of me, that cross my path. Everything has meaning when you're on a journey.*

"It's still a little high," she said when I picked up the call from my weight loss doctor a week after my second blood test.

"My white cell count?"

"Yes. Please get the last bloodwork you had done from your internist and have it sent to me. I need to see a baseline."

I realized I hadn't been to see my regular doctor in two years. My older daughter was right. I needed to see my internist. I made an appointment with him for a checkup. As doctors are apt to suggest to people who seem completely healthy and have no physical complaints, he said, "I'm sure it's nothing."

CHAPTER 28

YOU CAN SCREAM IF YOU WANT

It was a beautiful summer day. My older daughter had just booked her ticket to come to New York for a visit. I owed her some good, quality cough-free time. My trip to see her in Los Angeles a few months prior in March was not what we had hoped. She had been right; I shouldn't have gone out there to see her. I had spent most of my time in bed.

"I can't wait to come home," she said.

"Thank you for taking such good care of me when I was in LA this spring," I said.

"The parental tables have turned," she said.

"It was just a bad cold," I told her. "I'll let you know what my internist says. I'm getting another blood test today. It's the third one. I hope it's the last." I switched topics to more happy thoughts. "I want to show you the new house. It looks like something from *Ancient Aliens*," I told her, knowing her proclivity for all things mysterious. "Circles have incredible meaning," I reminded her. "It needs a lot of work, but you'll understand why I love it the minute you see it."

"I heard," she said. "It's kind of like the one in your Slim Aarons photo."

"Yeah," I said. "This was all meant to be. Sometimes I think I willed this house into existence."

"Maybe you did."

"It's weird," my internist said.

"What's weird?"

"There's something wrong with your white blood cell count, and it's weird. You need to see a hematologist."

"What? When?"

"As soon as possible."

"Can you tell me what you think it is?" I asked.

"Your lymphocyte count is too high, which means you could just be fighting off an infection, but you should get it checked out."

I mumbled an "OK," and he gave me the names of two specialists to contact. The first didn't have an available appointment for two months. I couldn't wait that long. The other could see me the following week. My older daughter had arrived from LA by this time and, along with my younger daughter, we went to see the hematologist, not knowing what to expect or even what was going to happen at the appointment. I was glad they were both with me.

"Don't worry," I told my children. "I feel fine. I'm on a new diet from my other doctor. It's that cold I got from moving. It's still lingering. I'm sure of this."

"Hopefully," they said without a trace of optimism. I recalled a time a few months earlier when my daughter had pointed to a large and dark bruise on my thigh. "What happened?" she had asked. "I don't know," I'd responded. This wasn't an uncommon occurrence.

"We Googled 'too many lymphocytes in the blood,'" my older daughter said. "Sometimes it's a symptom of blood cancer."

"I Googled it too," I said, "and it's also a sign of an infection, like from a cold, so I'm not worried."

"Colds don't last seven months," my older daughter said.

"The doctor said your tumor was growing for about three months before you felt it. Things take time," I said. "The body works at its own pace."

"You're not making any sense," my older daughter said.

"What do you mean?"

"It's completely different."

We were led into the doctor's office, where he was sitting behind his desk, drinking a Diet Coke and brushing away the crumbs from a just-consumed sandwich. He pushed his glasses to the end of his nose and read several pages of the lab report sent to him by my internist. He said that it wasn't very impressive, in an attempt to put us at ease. We were staring at him like deer caught in headlights. My older daughter whispered in my ear that doctors should know better than to drink a Diet Coke, and maybe we should look for another one. "Maybe," I whispered back.

"Your white cell count is off, but not to the point where I would even diagnose you without a test. You need a bone marrow biopsy," he concluded.

My older daughter burst into tears.

"Ok. When?"

"Now."

"Oh, I'm not really prepared for this now," I said.

"Why not? It will take ten minutes. You can either do it now, while you're here with them," he said while gesturing to my girls, "or you can come back, but you need it done."

"Does it hurt?"

"Yes. It hurts. I'm going to stick a needle through your hip bone and extract bone marrow. You can scream if you want, but you can't move."

OK. He's got a sense of humor, I thought, and appreciated that he was honest while trying to lighten the moment. I looked at my girls,

141

holding hands, my younger daughter consoling her older sister, who had begun to panic. They nodded.

"Let's do it," I said.

He led me into an examination room and told me to pull down my jeans to my knees and lie facedown on the table.

"Should I take my shoes off?" I asked

"I'm not going to touch your feet," he joked.

The doctor pushed hard on my lower back trying to find a place where he could stick a long needle through me and into my hip bone. When he located the place, he asked his assistant for a sharpie and marked it.

"I'm going to inject local anesthesia," he said. "We'll get you as numb as we can."

All of a sudden, I heard a scream from the doctor's office where my daughters were waiting.

"They probably just Googled 'bone marrow biopsy,'" I said.

"Then they should know you'll be fine."

The doctor cleaned my lower back with Betadine multiple times and draped a paper sheet over me that left only the area he was working on exposed. He left the room.

"Don't worry," the assistant said.

"Does he do this procedure a lot?" I asked.

"Yes," she said. "He's one of the best."

After giving the anesthetic enough time to do its thing, he came back into the room and told me to lie still.

He emphasized how important it was for me not to move. I felt his finger pushing on my back, then he inserted the long needle through my hip bone with a strong, swift plunge.

It's not so bad, I thought.

Then he began to suck out my marrow.

"Don't move, don't move," he chanted slowly and forcefully as I let out a blood-curdling scream.

"OK," he said, "we got enough liquid; now we're going to take a sample to biopsy."

"All done," he said as the assistant put pressure on my back to stop the bleeding. They bandaged me with a giant lump of cotton and told me to roll over on my back and keep pressure on the bandaged area. They said they'd come back in twenty minutes to check on me.

"Can my daughters come in?" I asked

"Of course," he said, "but don't sit up. Keep pressure on the wound."

"I won't move," I assured him.

"I'm fine," I said as they came into the room to sit with me. I saw their red, swollen eyes.

"We heard you screaming," they said.

I drove home to show them how OK I was. "I'm fine, I can drive. No worries," I said.

When we got home, I walked in the front door and crawled into bed. I wanted to turn on the gas fireplace and stare at the flames. I wanted to subdue the anxiety that was about to overcome me by focusing on the fire. But we had run out of propane during the winter, and the fireplace wasn't working. *I'm starting to hate this rental*, I thought.

"I'm going to nap," I yelled to my daughters who were in the kitchen making tea. I buried my face in the pillow and breathed deeply, with purpose, and forced myself into a state of calmness.

CHAPTER 29

YOU'RE GOING TO DO GREAT

I waited for my son and his good friend from high school to arrive. We were meeting for dinner at a favorite Italian restaurant on the Lower East Side. They got there as I was finishing a phone call that I had answered while waiting at the table, sipping a glass of red wine.

The call took less than a minute. It probably took less than thirty seconds in actuality. It was the end of the day, and the doctor was going down his list, like a grim reaper, letting his patients know their test results.

"Hello," I answered.

He got right to it. "OK. It's CLL. You're going to do great. Come back in two months."

"Um. OK."

"OK. Bye now."

And that was it. This was my diagnosis. That was the call that would define something about me for the rest of my life, however long that would be. I didn't really know at that point. I had more questions than answers.

I turned to my son and his friend and said, blankly, "I have leukemia."

"Oh shit," they said almost in unison. I saw the shock in my son's eyes.

There was silence.

"Let's get a bottle of wine. We need wine," I said as upbeat and joyfully as I could. In an attempt to reassure him, I said, "Listen, the doctor said I am going to be fine and not to worry. And I don't even need to go back to him for two whole months, so it really can't be that bad. What do you feel like eating?"

We finished two bottles of wine with dinner and never mentioned the call from the doctor or the diagnosis again. I was surprisingly calm. I felt safe, somehow. I felt like this was going to be good in some way, just like the doctor said—that something very positive would come from this. A feeling of relief, not panic, was enveloping me. *At least we know something now*, I thought. I went home after dinner and emailed my mother and sister.

The entire body of the email was just three letters: CLL.

I woke up for the next three nights in a row at around 4:00 a.m. I couldn't get back to sleep. I worried that I was going to be exhausted and assumed it was stress. I didn't feel stressed, but maybe my body knew something I didn't. Maybe all of the old stress along with the new diagnosis was floating around in my veins. I hated waking up in the dark. I didn't know what to do. I struggled between turning on the TV or trying to fall back to sleep. I felt paralyzed under the covers, waiting for the sun to rise with its permission to get up.

I thought of a former Buddhist monk that I had met at a book fair. He had written a book on darkness. I remembered what he said about waking up in the middle of the night.

"I get up and take a walk about 2:00, every morning," he said.

"Aren't you afraid?"

"When people see me walking on the road at 2:00, they think *I'm* the bad one, so I'm mostly avoided and left alone."

"The incandescent light has changed our circadian rhythms," he said. "Once upon a time, before the light bulb, people went to sleep just after dusk, slept for four hours, got up and did chores, work, or creative things, then went back to sleep until the sun rose. Those waking hours, between the dark and daybreak, are called the Hour of God. Great things happened during the God hour. Symphonies were written. Art was created. The Declaration of Independence was mostly written during the God hour. It's an in-between time where we're most open and vulnerable. We're able to tap into our creativity. The channels are open, and we are moved by our spirit to unexpected and immeasurable results."

"When you wake up," he said, "sit up or get up. You don't have to take a walk outside. Write in a journal, work on a creative project, paint, compose, or ponder the night, but don't fight it," he suggested. "Thoughts will come to you. It's a magical time. We're hardwired to sleep in shifts. It's natural."

I didn't want to wake up and write. I wanted to sleep and heal. I wanted a full night's slumber to cut my lymphocyte count back to normal. I wanted to fight off whatever was causing this. I had faith. I believed in the God hour, but I wasn't writing a manifesto or creating the next groundbreaking piece of art. I was scared. *No*, I thought, *I can't get into the habit of waking up at 4:00 a.m. and journaling.* On the fourth night, I woke again at 4:00. I sat up, like the former monk had instructed, but instead of writing, I talked to the darkness.

"Hey," I said. "I am alive and awake and here. I want to live and thrive and be healthy. I want to see my children grow old and have children of their own. I want to bounce a grandchild on my knee. Keep me alive. Help me fight this. If you could keep me alive until I'm somewhere in my nineties, that will be enough time for me here on earth. I'll be ready then to get rid of my body. I know I'll still exist as energy and consciousness, but I'm not ready to get rid of the physical me yet. Help me, please. Help me," I begged.

I sank back into my pillow and fell asleep. This was the last night I woke at 4:00 a.m. The monk had been right. I felt like my angels finally had a request they could accomplish.

CHAPTER 30

HEAL YOURSELF

Everyone I told about my diagnosis had a suggestion. One friend, I can't even remember who, told me to get a book called *Getting Well Again*. It was one of the few useful suggestions in a blur of information. The advice came at lightning speed, and most of it felt empty—the words of people who wanted to feel like they were helping when they had no ability to help.

"You should get more sleep."

"Exercise. You can literally work it out of you."

"No meat. No dairy. But you can have egg whites."

"I know a doctor who will give you infusions of vitamins."

"A green juice every morning will cure you of everything."

"Stop coffee."

"Sugar is the enemy."

"Get a blood transfusion. Keith Richards used to do this to get sober, or so I was told. It can clean your blood."

But the book was one of the better ideas. It was on Amazon. I downloaded it on my Kindle. *I'll start here*, I thought.

The online blurb about it said the book was a classic from the seventies. The couple who wrote it were pioneers in mind-body medicine. They taught that a person can almost think their diseases away. Their patients lived longer than expected. Some went into remission or were totally cured. The mind is a weapon in fighting disease, they believed.

I'd like to weaponize my mind, I thought. But I couldn't even say the name of my disease. I was afraid to utter the four syllables that made up the word: Leu-ke-mi-a. I thought if I said it, it would make it too real. If I uttered it even to myself, it would mean I was acknowledging its presence. I wanted to ignore the finding. I wanted to push it back in my mind and let it lie dormant. This is the problem with medicine today, I tried to tell myself. My diagnosis was an "incidental finding." In the 1800s, no one would even know they had this. It wouldn't be an issue. No one would have to worry if every little twinge, itch, or pain was your blood getting ready to spoil. (I ignored the fact that this also meant, in the long run, more pain, suffering, and death.)

The book said to visualize your cancer leaving your body. I sat quietly in my room, waiting for a vision come to me. I remembered sitting on the front porch of my childhood home with my Aunt Nell, shelling peas. She had the unshelled peas in her lap, nestled in her apron. The fresh peas were thrown into a bowl at her feet. I visualized her picking the extra lymphocytes from my blood and collecting them in her apron, like she was harvesting berries. I wished I hadn't seen a doctor for weight loss who'd tested my blood. I wished I was ignorant to what was happening inside my body. I wished, once again, that I could turn back time.

Getting Well Again was in good company, I noticed, from the suggestions that appeared on Amazon after I bought the book. *There's a lot to read*, I thought. *I need more perspectives. I need to hear more.* I wanted to know what therapists, caregivers, patients, and mystics had to say. I wanted to know if angels intervened, if hope prevailed, if positivity was a drug. I needed to read about people whose terminal cancer disappeared because they willed it away with a cocktail of hope and flat-out denial. Denial. That was my drink of choice now.

I read a story on Facebook about a woman who had an out-of-body experience while in a coma, met her father on the way to heaven, and got sent back because it wasn't her time. She opened her eyes while in the intensive care unit, tubes and machines hooked up to almost every one of her failing organs, and came back to life. She completely recovered over the next several months. *Miracles happen*, I thought.

I scrolled my Instagram feed for inspirational quotes, which I saved, edited, and put in an album on my phone to read when I needed a boost—a reminder of hope and words of wisdom. I Googled my disease relentlessly to find survivor stories. I read about a man who said he cured himself with a routine of vegetable juicing and exercise. I bookmarked the link and added it to my favorites bar. I stalked message boards and monitored a forum from England where people described their symptoms in great detail while all noting that these same symptoms could be from stress, exhaustion from work, or just aging. Their blood said, "You're sick with something that there's no cure for," but their minds and bodies said, "Life goes on and you could be a lot worse off." A lot of them had the same symptoms, the same complaints, and the same frustrations—tiredness, swollen lymph nodes, bruising, frequent colds, aches, and pains. "These are my people now," I said with a hormonal rush of pride. I wasn't alone.

"I'm here," I said aloud to the faces on my computer screen. "Keep talking, because I need to understand what's happening to you so I know what's happening to me."

"You give me strength," I told the photo of a woman named Marie who said in an interview that she was finally able to recognize her symptoms and deal with them.

Alex said he was tired but, then again, he told the interviewer, "I'm eighty-seven years old."

Jane could only garden for half the day instead of all day, and Diedre stayed positive by reminding herself that there were people sicker than she was.

Len was pissed off. "Yeah, Len," I said, "I'm with you. I wished I had never gotten that blood test. Knowing something you don't need to is its own kind of trauma. Fuck this shit, Len. Knowing sucks. And now, you don't think you can get long-term travel insurance, so you're grounded. Your wings are clipped, Len. I truly understand," I said with all the compassion I had.

I can learn from Len, I thought. He was brave and open and honest about hating this disease. He was frank about how pissed off he was that a blood test redefined how the world looked at him, how he was now a sick man that felt fine.

I tuned in every day to websites, forums, and message boards to read and reread. I watched them with the enthusiasm of a new season of *The Real Housewives of Beverly Hills* and my other Bravo reality show addictions. I watched a video made by a man who was no longer in remission and was about to go on another round of chemo. He was pretty sure it would work again. He was trying to gain weight before the chemo made him nauseous and unable to eat. I loved his perseverance and proactiveness. I rooted for him. "Eat what you want," I said aloud as if he could hear me through the computer. "Eat your heart out."

I read the story of someone who didn't tell his adult children that he was diagnosed as he didn't want them to worry. They had enough on their minds with their own jobs and families. He told his doctor that if he could be kept alive until he was eighty, he would die a happy man. He made it to seventy-seven. I read story after story about people who kept their disease to themselves as they didn't want to be seen and/or defined as "sick." They wanted to preserve normalcy for as long as possible. As I began to realize that the skinny man who needed to gain weight had been living with this disease—my disease—for seventeen years, and was more worried about what his wife would think if he became too thin than about how he would ultimately feel, I felt a swell of appreciation for the strength of others.

A woman with children was worried about the exhaustion that was a common symptom, so she was sharing her system for cooking and organizing meals for the family. It was well conceived, and she thought others could benefit from it too. Online, everyone had the same preoccupations. They were like a coffee klatch, sharing their tips and tricks for survival like they were swapping recipe secrets and crafting ideas. I admired that what brought these people together in the same virtual spaces was their desire to help each other, to listen, and to share.

It made me think about my conversation with the sister missionaries. They were right, I knew. They said that God would save me. The God that I was witnessing in the forums, sites, and message boards was the God of human compassion, care, and kindness. I saw God in the details of helpfulness and shared experiences. It was a more human kind of Godliness, born from suffering and the desire to live. I thanked the God of my youth and upbringing and the Gods of helpfulness, love, and care that spoke from the ether to whoever needed to hear their message. I picked up the pile of wet tissues that I'd thrown to the floor as I scrolled and read for hours. My eyes were red and swollen, and I could barely see through my tears.

It's time to close the laptop, I thought.

CHAPTER 31

I CAN SMELL CANCER

The fragrance store on East Fourth Street in New York's East Village was filled with large apothecary-style bottles of pure essences. Each bottle had a long dropper attached to the side for blending custom scents. The process for creating your own fragrance was to smell every pure essence and pull out the ones you wanted mixed together to create your own special blend—one that you could even name. The blender would keep the secret formula on file so when you ran out, you could just call for a refill.

My daughter wanted a fragrance that reminded her of Grandma's house, the home where I grew up that she loved to visit. The scent, we agreed, was a combination of clean laundry, houseplants, old newspapers, magazines, beeswax, chocolate, burnt toast, and vague seventies musk. I found it funny that there were no fragrance notes of a home-cooked meal, cookies baking in the oven, or an apple pie cooling on the counter. There was always a candle burning in a small glass votive, and chocolate could be found in a small bowl or dish somewhere in the vicinity to be picked at throughout the day. Plants, herbs, and flowers from a farmer's market or green grocer were arranged on the kitchen counter, adding color and life to the scene.

In the end, it took about eight bottles of essence to make our fragrance.

"The smell of my grandmother is the best scent in the world," said the woman behind the counter. "It's the reason I do this now. I wanted to make her scent so she could always be with me."

"We understand. We're doing the same thing, in a way."

"Before I opened the store, I was a nurse, but I had to leave. I couldn't do that anymore."

"Oh. Why?" I asked, wondering why she would leave a nursing job to open a tiny fragrance shop in Lower Manhattan. *She probably doesn't even have life insurance anymore*, I mused.

"I can smell cancer."

My daughter gave me a little nudge, out of her view.

I leaned in, to get closer to her. To get into range.

"You can smell cancer?" I repeated.

"Oh, it's terrible. Sour. Yuck," she said as she stuck out her tongue and made a face.

I continued to lean in over the counter to get as close to her as possible. I think she thought I was trying to see the secret fragrance formula she was writing down on an index card. She pushed the card to the side and moved away from me.

Smell me, I thought. *Smell me and tell me what's wrong.*

When we left the shop with our custom-blended scent that was really nothing like the scent of my mother's house but would now be the stand-in for it, I said to my daughter, "She can smell cancer."

"I thought you were going to fall over the counter trying to get her to smell you," she said, smiling.

But she didn't. She couldn't smell it. My cancer was undetectable to her. *This could be good news*, I thought.

"Maybe it's not that strong yet," I said with hope and optimism.

Things began to sink in. In the face of my diagnosis—as I dealt with shock, dismay, sadness, fear, and the specter of a future not anticipated or desired—I was calm and collected. I wondered if this was the result of my meditation practice. *Stay and play*, I reminded myself.

I freaked out more about a spill or stain on a rug than I did about having a type of blood cancer. I was oddly composed. I was surprisingly OK. I felt in control of everything. I felt a new strength and certainty. I wondered if I could assert my condition and make it work for me instead of against me.

But the fact was, I was idling, like a car at a stop sign. My foot was on the brake, waiting to take off when the coast was clear. My hands were at ten and two on the wheel. Safety was still important. I didn't get the kind of diagnosis that caused you to want to go skydiving—to fuck it all. Wait and watch, I was instructed.

"This disease progresses slowly," my doctor said.

"But time flies," I told him. "I have so much to do."

"Come back in six months for another blood test," he replied.

"So I need to live my life in bursts of six-month intervals?"

"You can come in every two months if you want."

"That's even worse," I told him. "At least I have a chance of forgetting about it over six months. If I have to come every two months, I'll never get it out of my mind."

I pushed myself to be grounded, so composed and rational, because I knew that I would make myself sick if I lost control. I needed to channel the happifying chemicals that lingered in my brain and release them into my blood to calm things down, to speak to the lymphocytes that were out of control and reproducing at an abnormal rate. I needed to reconcile the possibility that I might never need any kind of treatment, including chemotherapy, or I might need it next month. Next week. Tomorrow. *I am straddling two worlds again*, I thought. *One where I am healthy and well and one where I am sick and getting sicker.*

CHAPTER 32

THE THING

"I'm calling what I have 'the thing,'" I told my daughter. "I can't give it power, so we can't say its name."

"I understand."

"This is the only thing in my control with this disease. I can't let it win. I can't give it energy. I need it to get out of my psyche and then maybe it will leave my blood. I know the doctor said there's no cure, and that he's never seen a case of spontaneous remission, but I'm determined to be the first," I said.

"I have this thing," I told my guru in a one-on-one discussion.

"Tell me about this thing," he said.

"It's my blood," I told him. "I have too many lymphocytes. This causes stuff to happen to me. I get a lot of colds. I bruise really easily. I get exhausted for no reason. Sometimes I have muscle aches and pains. Sometimes my skin itches so badly that it feels like I have worms crawling beneath its surface. My immunity is compromised. I can't travel to places like India, with you, where I could get sick. I can't fight infections as well as before I got this thing. My body fights every day now to keep it at bay. I can't take my immune system away from the job it needs to do. I can't change its focus to something else, like a virus."

"Does the thing have a name?" he asked.

"Yes. But I don't like to say it. I'm afraid to say the name of it. I feel like if I say it, then I have it."

"Then just say 'next,'" my guru said.

"Tell me what you mean?" I asked.

"Move on from it," he said. "It sounds like you already have to a degree. See the doctors you need to see, then just say 'next' and keep going. Live your life."

"Next," I repeated.

"Next," he confirmed.

But saying "next" proved not to be so easy for me.

"I have a pain in my right side," I told my daughter. "I'm really nervous."

"You need to see your doctor," she said.

"I know. It might be inflammation. I'm not eating as well as I should. I'm paying for it now," I said.

"You don't know that."

"You're right," I told her. "I'm worrying about something that I know nothing about."

The doctor ordered an abdominal CT scan, with contrast. I sat in the hospital waiting room drinking down a yellowish liquid that would help things show up more clearly to the radiologist who would be reading my scan. It took about ten minutes once I climbed onto the machine. I took several deep breaths and held them as directed by the voice that spoke to me through speakers.

"Your scan is clear" were the words on the text message I read from my doctor a few hours after I left the hospital.

I texted her the thumbs-up emoji.

"Hey," I said to my daughter. "All's well. They didn't find anything wrong. The doctor told me to take it easy for a bit and see if it gets better."

"Great," she said. "You know, it's good to be careful, but it's not good to panic over little things. Not every pain means something fatal."

"I know," I told her. "You're right."

But when I wasn't with her, I fell apart.

I lay in my bed and poked the spot on my stomach trying to see if I felt anything, trying to see if it hurt more or less than the last time I poked it.

I curled up in a ball on my bed.

I hugged my pillow.

I crumbled under the weight of my own uncertain future.

Then other things started to happen. I developed a pain in my left cheek and ear. I felt a burning sensation that came and went. I went back to my doctor who sent me to an ENT. "It might be your sinuses," she said.

I went to the hospital for X-rays of my head and neck.

I got the same text as before.

There was nothing wrong.

I was fine.

"Wait to see if it stops."

I sent her back the thumbs-up, again.

I was strong and brave when I needed to put on a face of survival for other people, and I was a little girl when I was alone—scared and tentative—imagining things that weren't really there, like a monster under the bed.

The good news I received from the doctor for the second time seemed to confirm that anxiety was getting the best of me. Each time I sent the thumbs-up emoji, my pains and sensations slowly dispersed along with the tension that ran down my spine and across my shoulders.

"Next," I said as I readied myself for meditation. I sat for a few minutes, quietly thinking about how I needed to be clear and intentional with my thoughts and actions, how I needed to be practical and rational and in control. It wasn't so easy to do this when something took me by surprise, when I felt overwhelmed and overcome by the enormity of life and death, when I became attuned to every unexpected or new bodily feeling.

Why I was tired when I had a good night's sleep.

Why my lower back hurt when I had done nothing to cause it pain.

Why my heart was pounding in my chest when I hadn't moved a muscle.

Why I was so...

Angry

Afraid

Panicked

Desperate

When I could be...

Resolved

Calm

Practical

Disciplined.

Choose your thoughts about things that you see or intuit or believe, I told myself. *Choose a perspective that helps you. Choose how you want to feel and how you want to proceed. You can do this. You have the power of perspective and you need to use it for your benefit. For your sanity.*

"Don't leave me on the roof, God," I prayed as I settled down to meditate and release some of the stress in my body that was causing me to feel things that didn't really exist.

The next time I opened up *Getting Well Again*, I read about Jerry. He was diagnosed with lung cancer that had spread to his brain. The day Jerry received this news, he quit his job, settled his finances, and then sat in front of the TV. Within twenty-four hours of giving up on his life, Jerry began to experience pain and exhaustion. He didn't respond well to radiation treatment and within three months, he was dead. Then I read about Bill, who had the same diagnosis as

Jerry. Bill kept working, took some time off to do things he enjoyed, joined a support group, and, after radiation treatment, was virtually symptom-free. *I want to be like Bill*, I thought. *I want to outlive any prognosis I'm given. I want to live my life, not wait to die. I don't want a precipitous decline to do me in. I want a miracle. I want to be a medical miracle. I want to be studied at every medical college and cancer institute. I want to be the epitome of hope and healing for other cancer patients. I'm out to prove that spontaneous remission is real, if you can just believe that it is. I need to be the version of me that fights.*

There were many versions of me I had come to know since my diagnosis. My moods, feelings, and prospects for a healthy, happy future fluctuated with every twinge, gas bubble, burp, and unexplained ache.

There was a version of me that collapsed on the floor with crippling anxiety, needing to be picked up.

To have my hair stroked.

To be told everything will be all right, baby.

To be cuddled in loving arms.

To be handed a cup of tea and told to drink it because it would make me feel better.

There was a version of me that said, "I've lived more than half my life by any measure, and if I die tomorrow, I'll be OK with that.

"I'll be OK with not fighting."

"I'll be OK with giving up."

"I'll be OK with not trying to take control."

"I'll be OK with crawling into bed and staying there until someone has to carry me out."

"I'll be OK with being numb and self-indulgent and just for once, in all my adult years, thinking only of me and my immediate comfort and concession to the inevitable."

There was a version that said, "Fuck this shit, I'm going on a meditation retreat in India," which was the one place my hematologist told me I might want to avoid.

There was a version that asked, "How did I end up in my fifties with this haircut and saggy boobs?" Maybe I deserved to just disappear from the earth and spare everyone from the catastrophe I had become.

I walked to my bathroom and looked in the mirror. My face was streaked with tears. I was sad for Jerry. I didn't want to end up like him.

I stared at myself. *Stop it*, I commanded.

I cried again.

Shit.

Fuck.

Why can't you get it together? I pleaded to my reflection.

I rinsed my face and tried to smile, tried to force happiness to appear.

What would Len do? I thought. I wished I knew Len. I didn't even know if Len was still alive, living somewhere in England, pissed off because this disease—our disease—was keeping him from traveling the world with his wife.

Why couldn't I be pissed off and face this, too, with fury instead of fear?

Why was I so pitifully sad and feeling sorry for myself?

Why, when I finally decided to step up and call for an appointment with Dr. O. Carl Simonton, one of the authors of *Getting Well Again*— the book I'd been clinging to—was I not surprised that this wasn't possible? I learned he had choked to death years prior while eating a meal at home.

CHAPTER 33

INTO THE LIGHT

I moved from standing in front of my sink to sit down on the edge of my tub. From there, I slid to the floor. Muscle memory had taken over. Then something happened. This familiar scenario, my body stretched out, my cheek on the tile, reminded me of that New Year's morning when I disappointed my family and myself, and it created an overwhelming feeling to get up—to rise. My eyes opened wide. My palms were flat on the floor, ready to push me up. I was breathing hard. It didn't feel right to be on the ground, for once. I was given a choice, or rather, something inside me finally made me aware that I had a choice, and in that moment, I decided that the parable of the man on the roof was not going to be my story too. I didn't want to drown. What I'd been looking for in the world around me—an invisible touch, a rippling curtain, an angelic intervention—happened inside me and lifted me to my feet. For the first time in over two years, I felt like I could walk upright again, head up, shoulders back, eyes open. There was a lightness that made me feel like my feet were barely touching the ground. My smile was real.

I wanted to revel in this new feeling of invincibility. I wanted to smell the air and dirt and the leaves and the grass. I wanted to feel the wind on my cheek and not the tingling that came and went with my anxiety. I walked outside. No, I floated outside. The dust from the road was illuminated in God rays that seemed to beckon me. "Walk to the light," they said. I followed the road toward the God rays shining down.

I remembered the inscription in my book from the medium. *Let it shine. Let it shine. Let it shine.* Someone had come through to me, I joyfully realized. I wasn't alone after all. I wanted to see what was at the end of the rays. I wanted to find a warm spot of perfect green grass filled with flowers and bunny rabbits and other little creatures that would soothe me and tuck me in for a nap while the sun warmed and held me. I imagined my lymphocytes traveling up the rays and disappearing into the universe. I walked and walked but I couldn't find their end. *That's OK*, I thought. *It's part of the journey. Maybe someday.* The air and the walk confirmed my feeling of peace. I saw myself as well again. The pit in my stomach was gone. The need to collapse on myself was gone. I was calm, serene. I was six feet tall again. I hated that I had been fluctuating between two states of existence. One minute I was weak and dying and on the floor. The next minute I was strong and resolute and fighting to live. I turned around to walk back home. *When I finish construction and move into my new house*, I thought, *I will never let myself collapse on the bathroom floor. I won't let sadness bring me down again. I can cure myself, not of the disease, perhaps, but of my self-pity and my indulgence of symptoms that don't really exist.* Or maybe they did exist, but I would cure myself of giving them power over me. I would tell them to take a hike. Get lost. Split. I would fight the hold they had over me.

I once again recalled my conversation with the former Buddhist monk. I asked him about leaving his monastic life. I asked him how he did it. I wanted to know what it took to leave the monkhood and seek a new life, the life that he wanted.

"One day I took off my robe and walked away," he said.

"That's it?"

"That's it."

"It's that easy?"

"Yes."

It was almost too obvious to believe. The monk stopped being a monk when he took off his robe. I never thought that it could be this simple to define change in oneself. To forge a new path. To instigate a new way of being. I finally realized that I'd had the opportunity and power all along to take off my robe, to lose the trappings of what I thought defined me. To let go. My failures, my sadness, my disease could all be removed as the vestments I wore, in order to reset my place in the world. I could alter my outward expression by just finding myself again. I knew from the monk that I could finally remove what dragged me down and freely walk away from the fear and anxiety that were running my life.

"I'm stripping," I told my daughter. "I'm taking it all off."

She looked at me with a half smile and a raised eyebrow, not sure what I meant. Not sure what she was about to see.

"But first, I have something to do," I said. "I'm going to the store to buy lobster. We're going to celebrate the right way this time." I imagined pulling the tender, plump meat from the red shell and dipping it in hot, glistening butter. A communion of past and present. A new covenant with myself. The circle felt complete. I could taste salvation.

Let it shine. Let it shine. Let it shine.

ACKNOWLEDGMENTS

I would like to thank the friends and family who encouraged me to keep writing whenever I broke down in tears at the telling of this story. You lifted me up when I faced self-doubt, time and time again. I kept writing because of you.

Thank you to the writer I met at a book fair and emailed hoping for advice, who kindly wrote back and told me it sounded like I was still on my journey and that I should keep going. I did just what you advised.

Michael Norton. You helped me see myself in a more loving light. I am grateful for your generosity and care.

David Hollander. You see structure, form, and style where others dare not tread. Thank you for keeping me focused on craft, voice, and the important emotional takeaways I wanted readers to understand.

Many, many thanks to Dupree Miller, Jan Miller, and Nena Madonia for putting up with me sending proposal after proposal and finally suggesting that I write a different book. And here we are, thanks to your kindness and unending faith that I had a story to share...albeit, not the one I was trying to sell you on. Thank you to Austin Miller and Ali Kominsky for taking on this book.

Thank you to Post Hill Press. You've put me in the expert hands of Michael Wilson, Debra Englander, and Heather King. I feel safe, cared for, and completely understood. This is what a true collaborative partnership feels like.

Thank you to my doctors and healers who keep me healthy and hopeful, and to the online health, wellness, and spirituality communities that I stalk, absorb, and take inspiration from every day. Don't stop sharing and posting. You are a lifeline. You are teaching me so much.

My heart swells with love for the Vedic teachers and meditators who have counseled, educated, and helped me realize that we are not powerless to our circumstances. Thom Knoles, Susan Chen, and Peter Spoerri: My gratitude is everlasting.

Most of all, I want to thank my three children for allowing me to share their story, which is inextricably intertwined with mine. Thank you for your openness in letting me expose myself as a mother, woman, fallible human, and searching soul. I know it wasn't easy for you to read certain sections of this book. You are generous and gracious.